Being Time

Being Time

Case Studies in Musical Temporality

RICHARD GLOVER,
JENNIE GOTTSCHALK, AND
BRYN HARRISON

BLOOMSBURY ACADEMIC
NEW YORK · LONDON · OXFORD · NEW DELHI · SYDNEY

BLOOMSBURY ACADEMIC
Bloomsbury Publishing Inc
1385 Broadway, New York, NY 10018, USA
50 Bedford Square, London, WC1B 3DP, UK

BLOOMSBURY, BLOOMSBURY ACADEMIC and the Diana logo
are trademarks of Bloomsbury Publishing Plc

First published in the United States of America 2019

Cover design: Clare Turner
Cover image © Jack Featherstone

A catalog record for this book is available from the Library of Congress.

ISBN: HB: 978-1-6235-6895-5
         PB: 978-1-6235-6494-0
         ePDF: 978-1-6289-2272-1
         eBook: 978-1-6289-2701-6

Typeset by Integra Software Services Pvt. Ltd.
Printed and bound in the United States of America

To find out more about our authors and books visit www.bloomsbury.com
and sign up for our newsletters.

CONTENTS

ACKNOWLEDGMENTS

All three of us would like to thank Kristine Healy for her insightful engagement with the text and the peer reviewers for their extremely useful feedback. We are also grateful to the composers of the works included for providing such a rich basis for this exploration. Jim Gardner, former director of 175 East was generous in providing information about the performances of James Saunders' *511 possible mosaics*. The authors would also like to thank Radio New Zealand for making this particular set of recordings available. Lastly, we'd like to thank Bloomsbury for their open-mindedness in taking on a project of this kind.

Introduction

Listeners to music listen through time. The sounds that they hear occur in a temporal frame, and the nature of that frame transforms according to the listener and the listening space. The listener is a complex aggregate of different histories and faculties. Cultural conditioning, acuity in memory recall process, concentration, and stamina all contribute to the manner in which any one person will have a unique temporal experience of a musical work. As Jonathan Kramer writes in *The Time of Music* (1988), "Music allows us to experience subjective time without having to remove ourselves from the time experiences we share with other people."[1]

What makes temporality a topic of interest through which to explore music? Our experience of the passage of time continues independently of the event of listening to music; temporality does not "begin" when music is switched on. Similarly, when we listen to music, we do not switch off the outside world; our perceptions of temporal flow in musical listening are a part of our wider awareness of temporality. However, the act of listening to music is a powerful scenario for bringing temporal awareness sharply into definition. We become aware of the changes, indentations, and transformations that our sense of temporality undergoes in response to the music to which we are listening. Music prompts us to develop an awareness of our own relationship with the passage of time, and of our own personal imprint or interpretation of temporality. In this book we will explore our own perceptions of temporality in relation to specific listening experiences, and suggest what it is in the music that shapes and conditions these experiences.

We would like to suggest several ways of approaching this book that may prove useful. Firstly, it is a meditation on the capacity of musical works to influence temporality. It is also, correspondingly, an investigation of musical behaviors that have an impact on temporality.[2] The multiple voices that emerge in the book through the chapters, postludes, and discussions operate as an extended (in both senses of the word) invitation to consider musical works as a subject, rather than as fixed objects. Finally, we hope that the content of this work provides evidence of the continued validity and utility of exploring particular works in depth and developing an ongoing conversation about them.

A series of encounters

While each of the authors has thought deeply about temporal perception in music, we did not enter into this project with any fixed assertions or conclusions. What we have set up instead is a series of encounters between subjects and musical works. These encounters, in their numerous iterations and variations, have revealed musical characteristics and personal tendencies that, taken in combination, have a significant impact on temporal perception.

We found that the act of writing the chapters and discussing the works with others necessitated rigorous self-reflection. The ways in which each of us responded to the challenges of this reflective process are evident in the unique style and voice of each author's contribution. However, our reflections are first and foremost about a reckoning with the temporality of a musical work. The use of existing recordings allowed the three of us to have common reference points, so that we could discuss the similarities and differences between our experiences of listening to what is apparently the same event. We decided that there would be no correct or incorrect interpretations of each piece's temporality; each person's experience was assumed to be true insofar as it could be articulated. However, as listeners, we were often faced with our limits of memory, perception, endurance, or tolerance; we became aware of the impact of those limitations on our own temporal experience and our capacity for articulating it. The discussions that were born out of the labor-intensive process of listening, writing about our listening experiences, and sharing our thoughts with each other were incredibly fruitful and fascinating.

The process of piecing together this book, then, was initiated by examining our own responses to certain pieces, and questioning how we each understand our temporal experience as impacted by these pieces. We have dug deeply into our own personal listening contexts and have each attempted to discern a sense of temporal flow as it transformed throughout the listening experience. From this point of reference, we identified and explored the types of musical behaviors that bring about those experiences.

The three of us are all practicing composers and listeners of new music, but we have set out to explore temporal experiences with the latter identity in the foreground. We don't regard this book as primarily being a study of experimental practices. Our primary interest here is in the ways in which time passes when its flow is shaped by musical works. But apart from an interest in temporality, our main point of commonality and the reference point that makes it natural to collaborate is an alignment with experimental music practices. The pieces selected for study cover a broad range of experimental practice, and, furthermore, not all of them sit squarely within its boundaries. But given our individual and shared interests, we feel that we have the most to offer when considering music which falls generally within our field of knowledge.

We have found that experimental practices offer a rich groundwork for considerations of temporality. To briefly list a few examples, the prevalent interests in extremity extend to duration, form, and perceptual thresholds. The broader ethos of asking questions within musical works and using sound to reframe that which seems familiar is highly conducive to reconsiderations of temporality.[3] In this project, we consider how compositional and interpretive approaches in experimental musics affect our own temporal experiences in listening. Our work here does not represent a comprehensive study of experimental music, of musical temporality, or even of the works under consideration. Rather, it is intended to promote deep, considered thought on the nature of our personal experiences of temporality when listening to these works. It is a triangulation between the works, subjectivity, and temporality, as much as it is a triangulation among our three points of view. It positions the listener as an active participant in the practice of music-making. First and foremost, in writing the book we set out to allow the experience of the music to take precedence over and above the composed instructions to the performer, or theories of temporality.

We are writing about specific works, specific recordings, and the specific listening sessions we have had with those works. This project does not deal in generalities. There is no statement that we feel can be applied to a generic short or long piece, or even to a "typical" piece by a particular composer; we steadfastly avoid conjecture, as the focus is on the specific and the individual. The most obvious features of a piece might be only incidental to our experience of it. Anyone with an experience of late Feldman, for example, will probably have some idea of the kinds of responses that will be relayed in the following chapter due to the repetition of similar materials over a long duration. But the subject of the chapter about Feldman is *Piano, Violin, Viola, Cello*, which, while evidently related to a larger collection of work, has its own particularities, in addition to the author's unique experience of it. The postlude to that chapter will offer up different experiences of the same work.

Correspondingly, we do not assume that there is an "idealized" listener. The book celebrates the diversity in listening capacities of all listeners and, as such, makes no assumption that specific musical works will necessarily provoke specific experiences for a listener (for instance, a listener who may be able to place all previous events in the sequence in which they took place, or who may be able to remember detailed local-level changes of each instantiation of a repeated action). As listeners, we each have different capacities for perceiving, recollecting, and time-ordering sound, and different levels of acuity in the perception of temporality. As authors of this book, we intend not only to acknowledge but to highlight these differences, and explore their potential to reveal nuanced insight into the individual listening experience.

We have produced the material for this book by diving into a series of listening experiences and then reflecting on those experiences. Through immersion and reflection, rather than more traditional analytical methods, we have learned a great deal about ourselves as listeners as well as about the pieces we are discussing, and we have built up a vocabulary of some of the types of sonic behaviors that have an impact on our sense(s) of temporality. There is ample room for further exploration through other pieces, other listeners, and other fields, and we would all welcome such studies.

Authors such as Jonathan Kramer in *The Time of Music* (1988) explore the relationship between musical scores, proportionality, and temporal perception. However, our book bears the hallmarks of texts such as Don Ihde's *Listening and Voice* (1976), which is a first-person exploratory approach to the role of the auditory in human life. We aim to explore our own temporal experiences in listening from a first-person, subjective position, and to draw out similarities, tendencies, and conflicts across different perspectives where they occur. Where we mention work by philosophers, this is to underline a poetic alignment of ideas, or to find a parallel with our own experiences in listening to these pieces, rather than to extend the wider arguments of those authors per se.

Aspects of autoethnography characterize parts of our work. We have each aimed to communicate reflexive awareness of our listening habits and predilections. However, there are no strict autoethnographical methodologies employed in the book; we felt that it was important to allow each author's narrative to emerge organically, in accordance with the musical topic of their chapter. We each utilize different terminologies, different listening methodologies, and—to some degree—different voices.

The book is intended as a contribution to an ongoing discussion, rather than an end in itself. It reflects and supports the turn of attention, in more recent musical discourse, away from the score and toward both the performer and the listener, and it embodies our goal of understanding more clearly how we, as individuals, listen and perceive. In accordance with our working method of listening, reflecting, and conversing, what we believe we have learned by sharing our subjective experiences will be the topic of the final two sections of the book. We can only begin to establish consensus or discover overlaps among our experiences.

Starting points and methodology

We decided early on that each of us would pick two contrasting pieces and write a chapter about each. The main criterion for choosing each work was that it should have made a lasting impression on us in terms of how it affected our sense of temporality. Two of the chapters ended up discussing two pieces that related to a single issue: Jennie's "Monoliths" chapter covers pieces by Laurie Spiegel and André O. Möller, and Bryn's "Musical Brevity" covers two pieces by James Saunders. The other chapters address works by Chiyoko Szlavnics, Morton Feldman, Toshiya Tsunoda, and Ryoji Ikeda. An additional factor that we considered to be important in the process of choosing the pieces was that we wanted the works explored throughout the book to be of significantly different length (the shortest track discussed is ten seconds, and the longest complete work is almost two-and-a-half hours long). We did not carefully coordinate our selection of pieces, but as a consequence of our different knowledge bases, listening experiences, and areas of interest, the eight pieces we chose form an interesting complex of aesthetics, techniques, and impacts.

This book is in large part about subjectivity and, more particularly, the *subjectivities* of each of its three authors. In each chapter, we have allowed plenty of latitude for the author to explore an extended encounter with a musical work or set of works. We also found that we learned a great deal about ourselves as listeners and about particular works by observing and discussing our coauthors' experiences of our chosen pieces. With this in mind, we used the chapters, which were written first as a type of primary source material that provided a basis for further discussion. Each chapter is written in a highly individualized way, which, like the listening experience itself, is responsive to both the musical work and its author. At the same time, one author's experience of their chosen work often serves as a reference point for another author's discussion of a different one, resulting in a rich dialogue that permeates the text as a whole. We draw on prior discussions whenever they are helpful, as well as freely using metaphors and extramusical references.

The process of writing this book took on a certain rhythm, and we developed a sequence of actions that enabled us to work through each section in a broadly similar manner. Once a chapter was written, the two authors who did not write it would both listen to the featured work(s) in the chapter and have a separate conversation with one another about their listening experiences and responses to the written chapter. Both the resonances among and differences between each of our experiences of the same works provided fertile ground for critical discussion. One of those authors would then write a short reflection—which we have called a postlude—on their experience of the relevant piece or pieces, which incorporated elements of the conversation about the chapter.

In Chapter 7, we reflect back, synthesizing comments from an extended comparative conversation with observations made in the chapters and postludes. It is a hall of mirrors approach: reflecting on reflections upon our original reflections. If we take this metaphor a step further, the pieces themselves also hold up a certain type of mirror to our own subjectivities. In our perceptual notes on each piece—often presented in the chapters with minimal editing—we are listening to ourselves listening. As we amplified those listening experiences through writing, repetition, conversation, and assigned written responses, our awareness of both the qualities of the pieces and our own qualities as listeners became more focused. We learned, sometimes with painful clarity, what personal histories and tendencies we had brought to the works as listeners.

Given the deeply subjective nature of these case studies, it was important to all of us that each author's individual approach was preserved. At times, the writing style is confessional, autobiographical, or analytical. Sometimes direct, often tangential, each chapter reflects the author's engagement with his or her own subjectivity in grappling with the (often thorny) issue of temporal perception. We have allowed each of our personalities to remain embedded in the text because we recognize that each listener's experience of time is constructed individually; temporality *is* subjectivity.[4] To homogenize the writing so that the chapters would become structurally and stylistically uniform would be to lose sight of the premise of the book: that insight is gained by paying attention to the particularities of an individual listener's experience.

Significant differences between the three of us, as authors, became evident as the content of the chapters and the postludes emerged. For example, Bryn's observations foreground the impact that the pieces had upon him as a subject and highlight his perception of his own ability or inability to process the available information. Richard, on the other hand, writes initially in more objective terms about the behaviors of each work, and then moves toward a description of its particular impact. He attempts to explore, in fine detail, how specific sonic and design characteristics of the music can transform listening and temporal experiences, and how these experiences accumulate throughout listening. In contrast, Jennie tends to associate her experiences with visual references. She sees the various temporal behaviors of the sound works in the mind's eye and uses those images to understand their various scales, patterns, and effects. This book is built around these different approaches and outlooks, and exploits their variability to reveal new insights.

Backgrounds of the authors

While this book does not address, in any comprehensive way, the broad range of practices that constitute the experimental music landscape, it would seem that it is the overlap between our interest in experimental music and our interest in temporality that has drawn us together as collaborators on this publication. However, there are also things that set us apart; we recognize and respect the distinctness of the backgrounds and experiences that we each bring—and that have brought each of us—to this project. In order to make some of these more explicit and provide further context for our forthcoming contributions, we will share some information here about ourselves and our musical activities.

As a composer, Bryn Harrison has a long-held fascination with notions of musical time. Throughout his twenties and early thirties, he produced a steady output of solo and ensemble works and, in the process, developed an individual approach to dealing with time as a circular and repeating entity. Many of his subsequent works such as *Surface Forms (repeating)* (2009) operate at a speed and density that cannot be easily or immediately apprehended; they gradually draw the listener into an experience of the passage of time. More recently, he has continued to work with cyclical structures in a series of compositions of long duration that includes the 45-minute ensemble works *Repetitions in Extended Time* (2008) and *Receiving the Approaching Memory* (2014) and the 76-minute solo piano piece *Vessels* (2012–13). Over the past three years, his compositional research has focused upon the ways in which memory operates in music. His 55-minute *Piano Quintet* (2017) draws on a world of vanishings, recollections, apprehensions, and remembrances. Many of his earlier ideas on musical time were explored in his doctoral dissertation, "Cyclical Structures and the Organisation of Time" (University of Huddersfield, 2007). He has presented papers worldwide on issues of temporality in his own practice and coauthored (with Richard) the book *Overcoming Form: Reflections on Immersive Listening* (2013).

Richard Glover's work employs sustained textures and slowly transforming sonic aggregates, revealing his tendency to focus less on time-ordering in musical experience than on activities taking place in the present. His compositional practice draws upon aspects of process music within minimalist lineages. He explores complex sonic outcomes through simplicity in construction, in which the individualities of performers are heard in their responses to often brief, plain instructions. In *Seventh Inversions* (2011), a chord very gradually moves through different inversions via a process that results in a clear sense of closure when the chord reaches its destination of root position. This kind of experimentation with gradual transition led him to pursue an interest in how listeners perceive surface detail in sound and how they comprehend gradual, iterative process in music. His piano pieces *Logical Harmonies* (2011) explore the nature of iterative, stepwise process and investigate how smaller, contained musical structures can prompt a shorter yet heightened experience of a temporality that responds to both the shifting surface texture and the gradual change in the harmonic structure of the music. These research areas have manifested themselves not only in Richard's creative practice, but in his published texts on the music of Phill Niblock, Éliane Radigue, and James Tenney.

Longer pieces such as *Organ Harmonies* (2013), in which simple processes unfold over longer durations, prompted further exploration of how gradual shifts in sustained environments can bring about increasingly defined shifts in our listening and temporal experiences. Out of this exploration, Richard developed an interest in how listeners experience temporality in sustained sound environments without clear reference markers and how they adopt more performative roles within these environments. Along with Bryn, he has documented his work on listening and temporality in *Overcoming Form*, in which he also suggests some ways that a listener can develop finer control over their perceptual awareness of both sonic and spatial environments through the experience of extended durations.

Jennie Gottschalk has not dealt directly and explicitly with temporal perception in her work as a composer, but it is a topic that she began to explore in her dissertation, *Perception and Actuality: An Application of William James's Experiential Approach to the Music of Alvin Lucier and Michael Pisaro* (2008). It is only in looking back over this work in relation to this project that she has noticed a significant point of resonance between William James' writings and her own conception of temporality, as stated in this passage:

> [S]o we see that in the time-world and the space-world alike the first known things are not elements, but combinations .... When we come to study the perception of Space, we shall find it quite analogous to time in this regard. Date in time corresponds to position in space ... [T]he original experience of both space and time is always of something already given as a unit, inside of which attention afterward discriminates parts in relation to each other.[5]

Jennie's tendency to visualize the aspects of a work that have an impact on her sense of temporal flow runs parallel to this association made by James.

After completing her dissertation, she began writing about experimental music on her website, Sound Expanse, and often reflected on works in terms of their temporality. This interest took a more focused form in a section of Chapter Four of her book, *Experimental Music since 1970* (2016), called "The perception of time." Here, she draws on analogies often made by composers with visual art techniques.

Individual approaches to the chapters

Differences in the chapters can be seen to reflect not only the background and interests of each author but also the particularities of the pieces themselves; some of the musical works have clear sections or transitions, while others are notably lacking in those features. Some pieces have little to no secondary literature written about them, while others are well within the scope of scholarly reference. Some of the works are notated, while others are electronic. Even among the notated pieces, we have chosen a variety of approaches, from direct reference to the score to relying solely on a listening experience.

Bryn's engagement with his chosen works was informed by his broader context of knowledge. Rather than trying to exclude outside voices in an attempt to convey the "pure," embodied experience of listening to these pieces, he has taken a more inclusive approach that acknowledges preexisting interests in concepts such as repetition and memory. Parallel to his approach to each of the works with a context already in mind, each of his chapters begins with a contextual overview. Quotations that were particularly meaningful to him in the process of listening are then interwoven among the perceptual reflections. To some extent, this mirrors his process of listening, which was characterized by fluid transitions between reflection on the music in the moment and reflection on the music's context in terms of existing literature.

Conversely, Richard chose to approach the listening experience as drawing directly upon his relationship with the sound, rather than contextual information about the music, or biographical information of the composers. In his first chapter, he aimed to separate his background knowledge when considering his listening experience, prompting a stronger focus upon the sonic material rather than searching for clues as to how it was made, or for sectional references in clock time. This certainly prompted a greater focus upon the detail of the instrumental performance as well. He took a different approach with the second chapter, in which he felt it was important to make the reader aware of the clock time durational proportions of the tracks.

Jennie chose her pieces based on the temporal disorientation they caused, and her approach to each chapter was both an attempt to orient herself and to explain that disorientation. In the first chapter, charts were used to provide orientation for herself and potentially for other readers, as well as to be reference points for the discussion that largely revolved around their various behaviors. In the case of her second chapter, the monolithic nature of a work required another similar work to enable a discussion via comparison, as colors might be compared in relation to each other rather than being described as single units.

While the six central chapters may seem inconsistent in their presentation, there was no singular approach that would have been an honest account of the listening situation, either across these works or among the three authors. The experiences they provoke and the questions they stir up have a direct impact not only on the observations we make, but also on the form, presentation, and style of each chapter.

Identifying themes among musical behaviors

As collaborators, we have found that, although we cannot identify everything that feeds into how we listen, we can increase our awareness of the ways in which we each interpret or process temporality. In writing the chapters of this book, we developed an in-depth, specific awareness of our responses to the temporalities of particular works. Through the process of producing the following discussions and responsive postludes, and in reading and hearing the overlaps and divergences between our responses, we learned about what was unique in each of our own listening processes and reactions. We became more familiar with our own limitations in terms of concentration and stamina, and developed facility at switching between various levels and directions of focus. We approached this project not as idealized listeners, but as specific people.

The subjective experience of the passage of time is neither entirely linear nor proportional; a listener might perceive duration expanding or contracting according to the musical material, or time traveling in loops, escaping on detours, standing still, or skipping forward and backward. Inevitably, the process of attending closely to temporality reveals the idiosyncrasies of the listener; discussions of temporality very quickly become discussions of one's own distinct, personal experience.

While we acknowledge the significance of aspects of subjectivity, it is worth underlining that musical works are still central to this study. It has become clear to us that certain types of sonic behaviors within these works tend to have an impact on temporal perception. Specific subjective responses to these behaviors cannot be quantified or fully understood, but having relayed that they occurred, we can engage in some meaningful reflection on the musical moments that brought them about.

One of the most immediate themes to emerge among the musical behaviors that we observed in our chosen works is a constellation of loops, repetitions, and patterns. Looking back at specific instances, we might ask questions such as: How is a musical pattern repeated? Is it an exact repetition? Is the repetition interrupted by other material? If it is a loop, what is the duration of the sample? What is the content of the sample? How many different elements does the sample contain? How many times is it repeated? How long does the whole repetition last? If repetition is not exact, how are expectations set up? How easy is it to track? Do certain patterns become easy to anticipate? Do they defy expectations? How frequently do they diverge? Does that divergence become expected? Does the listening become less focused over time as expectations are evaded? What kind of dynamic is set up between recollection and anticipation?

Related to these issues is another cluster of concerns around scale. Which parameters are limited, and which are at play? Does the limitation of harmony, register, or dynamic level create the sense of a shallow surface? Does it create an ongoing or elusive sense of comfort or security? In what parameter(s) is the activity taking place? How is the ear directed? Are changes subtle or dramatic? Is there a sense of directionality? Is there a change of direction in the short term or the long term? To use visual or mapping terms, what is the zoom level of the piece? Are changes microscopic or macroscopic? What is the rate of change? Are there any perceptible changes at all?

Other issues that come up are the reduction or overload of information, the degree of perceived freedom of the listener, the intensity of the music (whether through pitch, amplitude, repetition, psychoacoustic phenomena, or any other parameter), tension and release, the intent and qualities of silence, sectionality, surprise, and degrees of familiarity. The topics that are most pertinent to these particular works are discussed in more detail in Chapter 7 under the broader headings of "Form, Structure, Memory, and Repetition," "Duration," "Speed, Velocity, and Intensity," and "Subjectivity."

Further considerations

This project represents our first collective engagement with temporality through the exploration of specific listening experiences alongside discursive reflection, and will lead to further work that addresses wider concerns relating to listening and experiencing experimental, minimal, and other musics. We intend for the present discussion to prompt readers to explore their own listening experiences in relation to time, and with this in mind, points of access to the recordings have been made available at the Sound Expanse blog to complement the pieces discussed in each chapter. We hope that the dialogic approach to knowledge creation that we have taken in this book will be appropriated by other writers and transformed as necessary to allow a range of individual musical responses to contribute to wider understandings of how music is made and received.

Finally, although the title of our book may draw associations with the title of one of Martin Heidegger's most well-known publications,[6] it is related more closely to Bryn's solo piano piece *Être-temps* from 2002. The piece comprises repeated panels of sound, which tests the listener's abilities to recall and compare its musical materials. This music poses questions: How effectively do we compare different durations? How does the flow of time differ within each separate panel? It asks us to interrogate our own awareness of temporality and to explore lived temporal experience through the act of listening. To investigate our own listening is to investigate our own temporality.

Our exploration of temporality in music has been reflected in the way the book has been put together. As we quoted Jonathan Kramer at the opening of the chapter, "Music allows us to experience subjective time without having to remove ourselves from the time experiences we share with other people." This project is a shared experience between us, but each of us has been able to explore our own subjective relationship with musical time in the company of others who share the same fascination.

Notes

1 Jonathan Kramer, *The Time of Music: New Meanings, New Temporalities, New Listening Strategies* (New York: Schirmer, 1988), 165.

2 See Chapter 7 for a listing of many of these musical behaviors.

3 See John Cage, *Silence* (London: Calder and Boyars, 1971), 13 and Jennie Gottschalk, *Experimental Music since 1970* (New York: Bloomsbury, 2016), 1–2.

4 See Maurice Merleau-Ponty, *Phenomenology of Perception*, trans. Colin Smith (London: Routledge, 2002), 490. "We are saying that time is someone, or that temporal dimensions, in so far as they perpetually overlap, bear each other out and ever confine themselves to making explicit what was implied in each, being collectively expressive of that one single explosion or thrust which is subjectivity itself. We must understand time as the subject and the subject as time."

5 William James, *The Principles of Psychology*, vol. I (New York: Dover, 1950), 622.

6 Martin Heidegger, *Sein und Zeit* (Tübingen: Niemeyer, 1927).

CHAPTER ONE

Foreshadowing and Recollection:

Listening Through Morton Feldman's *Piano, Violin, Viola, Cello*

Bryn Harrison

Thirty years after its completion, Morton Feldman's last work *Piano, Violin, Viola, Cello* (1987) still seems radical in its approach to form and its handling of musical time. While there has been much experimental work created over the past three decades that deals directly with a reduction in materials and extended musical durations, there are few such works, to my mind, that are able to deal with notions of time so eloquently or as poetically. In this chapter I will discuss the ways in which the work confronts me with the limitations of my understanding and, ultimately, with my own sense of being.

The italicized sections below are transcriptions of notes taken during the hours spent listening to the piece. My notes are interleaved among more general reflections on the ways in which time can be seen to operate in this work. This interleaving occurred in a manner that happened to resemble the piece as I found myself moving between direct contemplation and broader musical issues. Where appropriate, quotations have been included from other authors as a means of expanding upon my own direct experiences as a listener.

* * *

The dense, closely voiced chords that open the work alternate between piano and strings, with both voices sharing harmonic material of similar pitch content and duration. However, I find the function of each voice is entirely different: the piano's attacks, with their transient qualities, are noticeably stronger than the strings, making marks in time, while the sustained qualities of the violin, viola, and cello appear to play through time, etching lines in space. Feldman is acutely aware of these timbral distinctions, and highlights their intrinsic differences. Meanwhile, the similarities in pitch content, rhythm, and register between the piano and strings result in an interleaving effect, like plates of glass placed on top of one another. Periodically, the order of the piano and string utterances is reversed, or reiterated with slight alterations. Any suggestion of a logical pattern is made redundant by the constant rearrangement of the same materials, which themselves have sometimes been varied.

This interplay of the near and exact repetition of single or two bar units promotes both familiarity and confusion, and I quickly become aware of my lack of ability, as a listener, to make sense of the experience. At first, I was on top of it; I could hear those slight variations, that moment of repose, the reintroduction of the same material, but now, less than three minutes into the piece, I am less sure. I am faced with a perplexing question, which manifests itself in constantly changing ways: How does what I am listening to now relate to what went before? What I am experiencing is utter confusion of the senses, which leaves me wondering where I am.

* * *

These opening remarks have come from a set of preliminary observations I made after one of a series of seminars on aspects of temporality in experimental music that I gave to students at the Escola Superior de Musica Catalunya (ESMuC) in Barcelona between October and December 2015. As a visiting professor, I had the privilege of teaching three-hour classes on two consecutive days each week. Wishing to take advantage of these longer sessions, I used the time available to play the class recordings of pieces of extended duration in their entirety. All of these seminars focused on music of the last forty years and, on more than one occasion, included pieces from Feldman's late period that last over an hour.

Following a session in which we listened to the Ives Ensemble's recording of *Piano, Violin, Viola, Cello*[1] from beginning to end, much of the discussion with the group focused upon the very nature of the experience of listening attentively to the 76-minute work, with many students purporting to share my own sense of disorientation. Although I could have asked the students to listen to the piece prior to the class, what proved to be enormously rewarding was the experience of listening together as a group, of collectively witnessing time passing. I chose works with which few students were familiar, and encouraged them to make observations of the music after listening to the pieces without following or analyzing the scores. When we did analyze pieces using the score, this was done retrospectively, with the intention of relating what could be gained theoretically to the experience of prior listening. The students responded positively to these sessions, and I went on to prepare further seminars that dealt directly with the phenomenological experience of listening to this music: we talked about listening *through* rather than listening *to* these pieces. We also considered issues of recontextualization and how, for example, repetition might be used to provide different points of orientation and disorientation for the listener.

In this chapter, I will explore these aspects further and consider how a listener's apprehension of time passing in *Piano, Violin, Viola, Cello* is formed in response to what Feldman describes as his "conscious attempt at formalizing a disorientation of memory."[2] As my understanding and appreciation of Feldman's late works has come primarily from the experience of listening to these pieces rather than through undertaking detailed analysis of the scores, I will draw on my own perceptual, subjective responses to listening to this piece and talk at length about the resultant sense of "memory disorientation." I have chosen to present my experiences as a series of personal encounters with the music to capture the experience of time passing, moment to moment. I have reflected on the difficulties inherent to the act of describing that experience and, at times, have found myself restating comments made previously. Since I aim to provide an honest account of the experience of listening through the work, I have resisted removing these duplications from the text. Indeed, one of the perplexing aspects of listening to this piece is that it relies largely on the interplay of that which is the same and that which is different. It is perhaps inevitable, then, that I should keep returning to the same thoughts, albeit in relation to a different moment in the piece. With hindsight, it seems appropriate that, as I have chosen to write about a piece that is mosaic-like in its construction, it is perhaps inevitable that the writing has ended up taking on a similar form. In the interest of clarity, I have chosen to present my own perceptual analysis in italics as a means of making this distinct from the context that supports it.

The last decade has seen an increasing number of publications on Feldman's work, and there are several excellent articles that cover certain aspects of these late works in detail. I have drawn upon some of these texts here, although a survey of the literature is beyond the scope of this chapter. I am indebted to Dora A. Hanninen and Catherine Laws, who have written so clearly and perceptively on the late works of Feldman, as well as to Brian Kane, whose excellent essay "Of Repetition, Habit and Involuntary Memory: An Analysis and Speculation upon Morton Feldman's Final Composition"[3] provides the only in-depth commentary on this work in English, to my knowledge. Additionally, in order to clarify some issues relating to cognition and perception, I look to the work of music psychologist Bob Snyder, whose book *Music and Memory*[4] offers particular insight. Beyond musicology, the work of anthropologist Tim Ingold has also been helpful in illuminating issues of temporal organization. His argument for "thinking through making"[5] has some resonance, I feel, with Feldman's through-composed "intuitive" approach to form and structure, and with my own thoughts on listening *through* this work.

My listening sessions, in preparation for writing this chapter, were separated by a period of several months. Although this gap occurred through necessity, with hindsight it seems something of a blessing, inasmuch as it prevented me from becoming overly familiar with the music. While it is inevitable that I should become more accustomed to the events of the piece with repeated listenings, one of the continually perplexing aspects of my listening experiences is that Feldman's sequence of events, nonetheless, always remains somehow slightly beyond comprehension. The way in which duration operates when I listen to this work is both fascinating and frustrating; it seems that one cannot fail to get lost in the intricacies of its creation. Time passes in unpredictable ways, coaxing and teasing the memory into making associations, providing false anticipations and, in a Proustian sense, making one forget, if only to remember.

While actively engaged in the process of listening, I made copious notes. Admittedly, this is perhaps not the ideal way to listen, since information gets missed during the act of writing and, conversely, events become solidified through the act of note-taking. When my mind wandered, as it does from time to time in music of such demanding duration, these points were also duly noted.

Some of the following observations might also bear relevance to the other works from the last decade of Feldman's life. Indeed, the uniqueness of Feldman's approach is such that these works elicit responses that are unlike any other music that I have experienced. However, it is important to note that, although other commentators have often described these pieces collectively—as if there should be one, unified perceptual response to these works—there are, nonetheless, important distinctions to be made between one long late Feldman piece and the next, in terms of the experiential perspectives they provide. Especially notable is the differing degree to which segmentation operates in these works. While single-movement pieces such as *Three Voices* (1982) and *String Quartet II* (1983) have high degrees of segmentation, works such as *Violin and String Quartet* (1985) and *For Samuel Beckett* (1987) sound as if they have been hewn from one piece of material, leading commentators such as Sebastian Claren to describe them as "monolithic."[6]

Piano, Violin, Viola, Cello might be described as somewhere between the two; the various materials deployed provide clear points of differentiation, but in a manner wholly different to that in evidence in *String Quartet II*. In the latter, each page operates as a "frame" that "contains" musical materials. Each set of pages contains clearly contrasting materials and can be registered aurally as being significantly distinct from the last. In *Piano, Violin, Viola, Cello*, materials are also varied and, in some cases, highly distinct, but they are presented in close succession. Often, short phrases will be reintroduced alongside newer materials, or older materials will be reintroduced in new ways. The pages of the score offer no specific structural framework for the piece, and repeated sections occasionally go back to the previous page. While specific discussion of the score itself is largely absent from the following perceptual descriptions, knowledge of it provides a deeper contextual understanding of the work and highlights intrinsic differences to the block form approach of *String Quartet II* in which one page of material contrasts starkly to the next. The specificities of the integration of materials and the resultant sense of recontextualization that this provides are discussed further in the observations that follow later in the chapter.

Over the last decade of his life, Feldman composed single-movement works of long duration, including nine works that last over ninety minutes. The longest of these is *String Quartet II* (1983), which can last over six hours without an intermission. Working with such extended durations puts issues regarding the form and structure of these works into question. Once the graspable limits of the duration of the work are perceptually out of sight, part-to-whole relationships begin to take on new meanings and the differences between those aspects of the music that provide proximity and those that create segregation are difficult to discern. What Jonathan Kramer describes as "nondirected linearity"[7] is supported by the use of a pitch language that is imbued with a sense of anticipation, but cleverly avoids the directional implications of functional, tonal harmony. Rhythm provides impetus while offering little indication of beat placement or meter. As Feldman has said:

> My sense of time had been altered, so intently focused was I on the way the music changed from note to note and chord to chord. It created a living, breathing network of relationships that extended across its length. You don't really listen to these pieces, you live through them and with them. By the end of the Second String Quartet, I felt it was living inside me too.[8]

This sense of the material "living inside me" might be said to extend not only from moment to moment but from piece to piece. Although each work establishes its own sound world, its own working processes, and its own internal logic, a workable harmonic vocabulary is transferred from one piece to the next and through changes in instrumentation. The language of the music does not change dramatically from one piece to the next. Rather, there is a rethinking of the situation, in a manner not unlike the late Beckett novels such as *Company* (1980), *Ill Seen Ill Said* (1982), and *Worstward Ho* (1984) in which the same vocabulary, the same place, and the same types of characters enact the same scenario but from a new point of view.

In the case of *Piano, Violin, Viola, Cello*, it seems to have been Feldman's intention from the outset to create the work from two distinct timbral components: that of the different instrumental groupings of string trio and piano. Indeed, not only do the strings operate largely as a unit, but rarely do they sound at the same time as the piano. This dynamic interplay forms much of the dialogue and rhetorical underpinning of the piece.

* * *

From the opening moments of the piece, the bowed string chords emanate physicality. The act of drawing the bow in broad strokes from left to right and right to left gives the closely voiced harmonies a feeling of breadth. Each of these chords enters uniformly and quietly, and is sustained without deviating in volume, filling the spaces left from the piano's decaying resonance. I am reminded of the sheer beauty of hearing strings resonating harmoniously, without the need for vibrato or additional coloration. Against this, the piano's chords are endlessly reactivated, the onset of each chord being strikingly different to the softer but persistent entries of the strings, despite their quietude. Although the register that the lower notes of the opening piano chords occupy are the same as that of the strings, the higher notes are noticeably separated, with the highest voices an octave above.

Immediately following the interleaving of these two parts comes a brief moment of repose, with the piano and strings playing a held chord together. Then the opening figures return with slight variation—the piano chords revoiced and the left hand notes in a lower register. Immediately leading on from this comes another brief point of repose, this time with only single notes on the strings.

What follow are short events that closely resemble the opening bars, but already the ordering feels different. Feldman's use of material is economical; right from the start, materials are being reintroduced, reworked, but in a way that is difficult to discern. Sometimes short, complete phrases are repeated exactly but, most often, they are left incomplete, so that endings feel like the openings of new phrases and openings feel like endings.

* * *

Both Hanninen and Kane have commented on this aspect of recontextualization in late Feldman. Kane, taking his lead from Sebastian Claren, says, "The discourse produces essentially a richer and richer accumulation of relations, details and distinctions within a single musical entity."[9] Hanninen, speaking in more general terms of the problems of recontextualization in late Feldman, writes, "Things change. Our perceptions of things change. Context changes our perceptions of things."[10] Only a few minutes into the piece, Feldman has cultivated a situation of multiplicities, a complex web of syntactical relationships between the new and the half-remembered. A space has been opened up for dialogue between that which is made active in the mind and that which resides in our not-too-distant memory. Feldman has described the piece as a "rondo of everything," saying:

> Everything is recycled. A lot of times it comes back just modulated a little bit, and that sounds very weird. Because you feel that it's the wrong notes. The fixed registration of the notes is like a stand and then the stand becomes a little bit blurred because you hear the pitches differently when they come back. There's just something peculiar about it.[11]

Hanninen, speaking of *Why Patterns* (1978), says, "recontextualization becomes a compositional technique; phenomenal transformation of repetition creates coherence and continuity, an autogenetic approach to musical form."[12] In *Piano, Violin, Viola, Cello*, materials are being introduced and reworked almost from the start, but in a way that is difficult to discern. Sometimes short, complete phrases are repeated exactly but, most often, they are left incomplete, so that the ending feels like the opening of new phrases, and the openings feel like the ending. This effect is wholly disorientating and becomes a recurring theme through this chapter.

✳ ✳ ✳

Four and a half minutes into the piece, the piano begins to play more widely spaced chords of varied harmonic content, seemingly at a slightly quicker pace. The pitch content is sufficiently varied to feel like a point of departure but not so different as to produce a distinct dislocation from what has gone before. What is more noticeable is a sense of opening up, of breaking away from the feeling of containment that has prevailed until now. Against the piano part, Feldman continually repeats a single, openly voiced chord on the strings. The simultaneous effect of motion and stasis is both stabilizing and unsettling, both anchoring and disorientating.

As this continues, I become aware of how Feldman continually revoices the static chord between the string trio. Although the pitch content remains unaltered, the assignation of instrument to the lowest, the middle, and the highest notes is constantly changing. As is characteristic of Feldman's compositional approach, each chord incorporates natural and artificial harmonics, which imbues each chord with subtle variations in timbre and weight. Sometimes the violin plays the highest note or, in other instances, it is the viola or cello sounding these as artificial harmonics.

As I become accustomed to this constant sense of variation within a single chord, Feldman brings in something new: an arpeggio, a single gesture consisting of a four-note piano figure spread over four octaves. Immediately the familiarity of the materials, which, until now, have consisted almost entirely of vertical relationships, is lost; the spell of an entirely chordal composition is broken. I realize in a moment that the piece can never be the same again; these single notes, spread out evenly across time, draw attention away from the repeated string chord and provide an entirely new point of focus. I register this as a distinctly new event but already Feldman has moved on, returning, albeit briefly, to the opening materials of the piece. This time each utterance is separated by a short pause, causing me to hear this material in a changed context. Did the arpeggiated figure mark a point of closure or an opening into an almost-familiar place?

I was going to say that what follows is a kind of alternation between the opening and secondary materials, but to describe this moment in the piece as a kind of alternation is perhaps a little misleading. The materials do interleave, but the relationship between them is complex and unpredictable, teasing the listener into observing false relationships and, in the process, taking me further and further into this enclosed sound world. I find that those moments that seemed to consist of differentiated materials now sound uncannily alike while, at the same time, I start to notice distinct differences between materials that had appeared similar to begin with. Registration does not seem to be the same thing it was five minutes ago; the occasional lower note played on the cello has a new vitality, a new significance. Events seem to be moving at different rates, and, already, my expectations have changed.

What opens up is a more active space in which I am encouraged to stop making sense of things and simply listen. Possibilities of what might follow arise momentarily, but almost always Feldman does something else. So little seems to have happened, and yet there are so many resources to fall back on: the opening material, the repeated string chords, solitary piano chords, silences, an isolated arpeggio. All of these elements are infused with the possibility of direct repetition or some micro-variation that always appears closely related. Through this complex web of interactions, a beautiful paradox comes into play: the music is wholly reliant upon memory and yet, with its insistence on each moment, offers no real opportunity to reflect.

* * *

In his book *The Percussionist's Art: Same Bed Different Dreams* (2006), percussionist Steven Schick speaks of this kind of affliction of memory in late Feldman. Discussing another late work, *Crippled Symmetry* (1983), Schick says:

the music seems to float forward in a perpetual state of balance between recollection and prefiguration. Listening to *Crippled Symmetry* evokes a forgotten vocabulary of memory: of foreshadowing and recollection, of being in and out of time…. A listener is left perpetually grasping for what *is* and what *was*, and both are tantalizingly just out of reach.[13]

Bob Snyder's perspective further illuminates this kind of listening experience:

It is possible to construct nonlinear music that makes use of primarily associative memory relationships. Although lacking linear progressions and "deep" hierarchical order, such music uses similar materials in different places to make associations across a piece. Its structure could be described as a "web," rather than a "line." Because it is non-progressive, however, at any given time this type of music gives listeners much less of a sense of location: the places where similar material appears are potentially confusable in memory.[14]

For Snyder, music that exists at the limits of this "nonlinear" approach enacts what he describes as "memory sabotage."[15] Feldman himself spoke of erasing the memory of what we have heard before[16] implying that, as we move from one event to next, the previous information must be stored in some incomplete form, only to be rediscovered and reencountered at a later moment.

✲ ✲ ✲

As I continue to listen, twelve minutes into the piece, I become aware of a change: the piece seems to be getting slower but also more spacious. Prolonged moments in which the strings are entirely absent begin to emerge, and the activity of instrumental groupings crossing over one another like plates of glass has been replaced by isolated piano chords. The register of these chords seems relatively contained but the pitch content feels freely chromatic. Feldman never allows the strings to go far out of sight; they are always somewhere on the horizon, and I anticipate their entry. What emerges is a constant state of coming and going between piano and strings; now the opening chords, followed by the repeated string chord, then the opening again.

The first isolated string event emerges approximately sixteen minutes into the piece: a dyad consisting of a minor seventh on the viola and cello, closely followed by an ascent in pitch played on the violin, two octaves and a minor third higher. This short figure is then heard again, but this time as a variation to the previous entry and with the highest note on the violin sounding a tone lower. This variation appears as an answering phrase to, or an echo of the first. This question and answer is repeated three times to create an eight-bar unit. I am reminded of how balanced and stable this sounds in comparison to the off-centeredness of the oddly paced phrases observed previously in the piece.

Immediately following this string passage, I witness what might be described as the first real motif in the piece: an isolated mid-range piano gesture. The similarity in pitch and rhythm to the string passage emphasizes its connection to the preceding event, but the effect is wholly different. Here the pitches are reduced to a single octave on the piano, producing a figure that is distinctly melodic in character. To emphasize this further, Feldman repeats the figure, unvaried, and then sounds it again, a tone lower. All of this has the effect of accentuating the melodic profile of the motif. I have heard the piece on several occasions before, but am just as taken aback on this occasion by the contrast of this event to the preceding ones, and its signification as a structural marker on what I am observing. There is something odd and possibly out of place about this gesture. Is this because it has fewer of the characteristics of the preceding material?

The materials open up once more with an alternation of string material and the more open, sparser piano chords. A variation on the isolated string chords occurs and then, for the first time, high individual piano notes against more characteristically chordal materials in the strings. These isolated piano notes become more prominent and create, for me, one of the most introspective moments in the piece. It is almost as if the piano is given a moment of privacy, which is quickly overshadowed by the return of the strings.

I am now some twenty-two minutes into the piece. Each event feels more separated, as if framed as individual moments in time. I am becoming aware that there are fewer new ideas being introduced. My relationship with the piece continues to change; my listening experience is becoming a site of remembrance, wherein previous events are continually revisited.

* * *

While taking notes for the above, I observed that in the process of documenting this passage, the reduction in the number of new events gave rise to the amplification of existing ones, as each repetition was brought back into conscious awareness, often after a significant period of time had elapsed.

Bob Snyder says of the act of repetition in music:

> When there is repetition present, each repeated occurrence of an element is somewhat like a rehearsal of its other occurrences.... Thus, in general, repetition greatly enhances chunkability, hence memorability ... Recycling a particular present ... can keep a particular chunk active in short-term memory, preserve its time order and details temporarily, and increase the chance that these will make it into permanent storage in long-term memory.[17]

In late Feldman pieces, repetition can be seen to operate on two principal levels, and the emphasis toward one of these types of repetition or the other varies quite considerably from piece to piece. The first level of repetition is principally structural and regards those whole sections of material that are repeated after a period of time has elapsed. In the case of a work such as *Piano, Violin, Viola, Cello*, this involves the reintroduction of particular phrases or blocks of material, while in other works such as *String Quartet II* it involves the repetition or near-repetition of entire pages of material.

The second level of repetition operates more on a micro-level and concerns the act of directly repeating a single unit by placing repeat marks around it. In *Piano, Violin, Viola, Cello*, Feldman makes use of this approach to repetition but, in marked contrast to many of his other late works, each passage that contains repeat marks is repeated once only. Feldman's principal interest here is in the first level of repetition: he continually reintroduces phrases and materials that differ in character back into the musical discourse, in order to manipulate the listener's perspective.

✳ ✳ ✳

The reordering that I am witnessing as I write seems to continue for a significant period of time. It is accompanied by what feels like a marked slowing down in the music. Has the piece actually slowed down, or is this the result of a change in my perception of time passing? It becomes difficult to tell.

Some twenty-eight and a half minutes into the piece, new material is introduced; what I hear is a closely voiced triad played on the strings, followed by two dyads on the piano. The first of these dyads sounds in the same register as the strings and is in marked contrast to the upward and downward movement of notes of the second triad. The effect is of an arrested moment in the strings, followed by a blossoming outward of the notes from the piano. The fact that this event is repeated after a short period of silence gives the impression of the string chord retracting, after which the piano notes open up the gesture again. Each time, the note values are varied slightly— keeping me attentive to those small changes in patterning and pacing.

What follows is a succession of previously heard materials. The piano motif, which I had previously described as sounding so striking and novel, appears again. Its reappearance feels just as significant as a structural marker but Feldman chooses to only repeat this gesture once—it makes its appearance only to become absorbed within the more general musical discourse. There is an overbearing sense of sameness in the constant interplay of all these materials, and yet Feldman has the uncanny knack of giving each of these materials a renewed vitality each time they reappear. Somehow they just don't sound the same.

Some minutes later (around thirty-seven and a half minutes into the piece) a distinctly rhythmic passage is introduced on the strings—a repeated figure consisting of two shorter chords of equal value, followed by a longer one. Each of the shorter chords has weight, as if tenuto markings had been indicated in the score. This event is interspersed with the piano materials heard previously but, again, the context in which these piano notes are heard has changed. What I witness is what Hanninen would refer to as an "estranged repetition."[18] Instead of providing a sense of blossoming, this time it is the rhythmic profile of the figure that I am drawn to, which seems to echo the shorter rhythmic values of the string chords.

Again, the music opens out and a succession of past events comes once more into play. It is interesting to note that even now, just over halfway through the piece, the opening materials are still reintroduced, albeit as threads or remembrances of what has passed. It occurs to me, momentarily, how the significance of these materials has changed over time. At the start, this material felt like an introduction, a means of establishing the directionality of the piece; it felt somehow solid and stable despite its ephemerality. Yet, hearing it now, I am not in the same place.

✻ ✻ ✻

This sense of return to the opening material that is discussed above is reflected in the writing of Kane:

> We, as listeners, are involved in the process of trying to assimilate ever new sense data—to test it, to spin it round, to place it into some order that will allow the inscrutability of all material to become clarified and legible—but, at certain moments, material insistently enforces its own dogmatism. We *return to the opening bar of the piece, having suddenly arrived nowhere and beginning again, but the new beginning is not the same as the old one.*[19]

Each return to the "start" is also a return to the last time this material was introduced and the time before that. This leads us to question the ways in which we remember these events and how we process the information we receive. Was I recalling the opening of the work when I heard this musical statement or the last time it was brought to consciousness, or some kind of amalgamation of all these past events?

✻ ✻ ✻

Around thirty-two and a half minutes, a chord is played softly by the string trio, and immediately afterward, two isolated A flats are played in succession on the piano. Then the whole phrase is repeated. These isolated piano notes evoke a strong sense of intimacy. The sensuality of touch that such simple materials can evoke is striking. I am reminded of what Feldman said of Mondrian not wanting to paint bouquets but single flowers at a time.[20] These two single notes convey so much eloquence. After a short alternation of piano and string chords, the event appears again and, once more, the solitary A flats reinstate their significance. Any slight significance that is attributed to any single event becomes magnified and imbued with meaning, but only to mark its own vanishing in the wake of another event at forty-four minutes and thirty-eight seconds: What follows is a series of quicker-paced passages that are presented as an alternation between the piano and strings. Each motif is confined to a pair of cluster chords, the second of which is higher in register. The difficulty I have in identifying the notes of the cluster and the sudden change of register draws attention to the rhythmic profile.

* * *

It is easy to talk about the parametric attributes that we are observing at this point as if we have just stepped into the piece without prior knowledge of all that has gone before. On the one hand, my aural faculties seem more acute at this stage of listening; I am immersed in this sound world and I feel as if I understand the conditions through which I am invited to listen. On the other hand, with this familiarity comes the possibility of not fully processing the information I am receiving. My sense of perception has become distorted through fatigue.

Is it that my recollection of a similar past event is interfering with what I am hearing now and creating a disturbed view of time continuity? I am certainly aware that the piece surpasses the limits of my concentration, and that the composition is larger than what I am able to comprehend. My perception of scale, it seems, is not just reliant on the sheer duration of the work, but is directly related to my ability to handle the information I am being given. As Catherine Laws has said of the work *Neither* (1977):

> Eventfulness is minimised, ironically, through the very realisation of the proliferation of possibilities; the internal reflection of material through contextual variation and juxtaposition gives the effect of everything being the shadow of everything else: the original image, if it ever existed, is beyond reach.[21]

This sense of things being "beyond reach" or "being the shadow of everything else" has a strange paradoxical effect; all the events that have taken place up to now seem also to have a nearness to them; it is as if anything that has gone before *could return* at any moment. This sense of things feeling *out-of-reach* and yet *close-at-hand* has a disconcerting effect: I feel lost, but with a heightened awareness of that very environment that I am lost within. The degrees of magnification of individual events appear greater, and yet these details are only available to me *at the time that they occur*, since I find myself unable to directly recall the previous occurrence of this event with any certainty. It becomes impossible, with such high information content and long overall duration, to say whether what I perceive *is* the same material as before or whether some slight variation has occurred. Snyder tells us:

> when we have any type of experience repeatedly, we have great difficulty remembering the details of any particular occurrence, unless they are fairly unusual. This is referred to as an "interference effect" and is based on the idea that similar memories interfere with each other. Interference effects are a direct result of the limits of categorization: we simply cannot retain all of the minute differences between different but very similar experiences.[22]

In *Piano, Violin, Viola, Cello*, this interference effect is felt not just as a result of having witnessed the same materials reoccurring, but from the confusion that arises from the ordering. The sequence of events follows no observable pattern and does not adhere to the principles of causality. We might say that form *is* created and *does* come into being, but arises through the process of writing, rather than being created out of some a priori design. Feldman has spoken on this, saying that he places his faith in intuition and that music shouldn't rely on formal processes and systems.[23] This is not to say that Feldman is suggesting that the act of choosing which event will follow is entirely random or chance-determined. It is clear that Feldman makes discerning judgments based upon the immediately preceding sequence of events but that these are not the result of some predetermined, organizational system; an alternative decision would have led to a different set of associations between the materials and thus a new set of contextual relationships.

Feldman's approaches illustrate that each event is entirely dependent on all the others that have preceded them. Each "spur of the moment" decision made by the composer becomes part of a chain of events; each intuitive decision is a response to another made by the composer previously in the piece. Theoretically, it would be possible to trace the evolution of the work backward, viewing each event as a ramification of the preceding one a different momentary decision would have led to a different sequence of events. I have described this elsewhere as a kind of *diary form*—a form that unfolds *out of itself*, through the real-time process of composing.[24]

Anthropologist Tim Ingold has written extensively on what he sees as "the study of human becomings as they unfold in the weave of the world."[25] In *Making* (2013), he states:

We are accustomed to think of making as a *project*. This is to start with an idea in mind, of what we want to achieve, and with a supply of raw material needed to achieve it. And it is to finish at the moment when the material has taken on the intended form … I want to think of making, instead, as a process of *growth*. This is to place the maker from the outset as a participant amongst a world of active materials.[26]

Ingold reflects at length upon the differences between *building* and *dwelling*, describing how the notion of building usually manifests itself in an architectural prior design, while dwelling is more transitive or the result of *being*. Crucially, he draws on the notion that *dwelling* emerges from the very process of working, whereas *building* presupposes the completion of the design of work prior to its execution.

A comparison might be made between this idea and Penelope Reed Doob's thoughts on the construction of mazes in *The Idea of the Labyrinth: From Classical Antiquity Through the Middle Ages* (1994):

Maze-treaders, whose vision ahead and behind is severely constricted and fragmented, suffer confusion, whereas maze-viewers who see the pattern whole, from above or in a diagram, are dazzled by its complex artistry. What you see depends on where you stand, and thus, at one and the same time, labyrinths are single (there is one physical structure) and double: they simultaneously incorporate order and disorder, clarity and confusion, unity and multiplicity, artistry and chaos. They may be perceived as a path (a linear but circuitous passage to a goal) or as a pattern (a complete symmetrical design).… Our perception of labyrinths is thus intrinsically unstable: change your perspective and the labyrinth seems to change.[27]

We might think of the designer of the maze, looking down on his or her immaculate, symmetrical design as being comparable to Ingold's notion of the architect or the builder, who takes delight in the abstract construction of its making. Similarly, we might think of Doob's maze-treader as Ingold's dweller, unaware, principally of the particularities of the construction of the maze but taking delight in the experience of confusion that comes from living *in* and as *part of* its design. The crucial difference, of course, is that the maze-viewer can see and appreciate the whole picture at once, whereas the maze-treader must discover the design for themselves, as a lived experience, born out of a sense of discovery and reliant on the passing of time and their constructed sense of memory. The maze-dweller, on the other hand, learns about their surroundings through a process of trial and error that is wholly distinct from the trials and errors that the maze-designer undergoes. Indeed, the classical symmetry that may be important to the maze-designer might not be in any way known to the maze-treader from their on-the-grid perspective. And yet, the proportional, symmetrical design of that particular maze still remains an intrinsic part of the experience of the maze-treader—even if an understanding of that design remains firmly out of reach. A different design to the maze would lead to a different lived experience.

Similarly, in Feldman—to borrow a phrase from Ingold—we "learn to learn"[28] from the very act of listening. *Piano, Violin, Viola, Cello* does not offer the listener a framework to guide them along the way, but, instead, it sets up an experience within which we learn to form our own narrative time. In some instances, our sense of anticipation—my sense of predicting what will happen next—is fulfilled, but just as often I get it wrong. Just as Feldman creates his own knowledge of the work from a process of *going along*, we too, as listeners, must build up our own understanding and appreciation of the work as it unfolds before us. Through this approach we build up our own perspectival view of the piece, while having to acknowledge that it is a view that is constantly changing, forcing us to reorientate ourselves constantly. As the contextualization changes so must we.

Brian Kane explains this further:

Feldman's compositional strategies present a unique formal problem: while suggesting the possibility of being read according to conventional narrative organization, the roles of key musical signifiers shift as the piece unfolds and produce an inscrutable logic of development that is simultaneously motivated and ambiguous.[29]

Clark Lundberry, discussing photographer Steven Foster's relationship to Feldman's work *Triadic Memories* (1981), has articulated similar responses:

For there is, built into one's very hard-driven desire *to be* present—and to pay attention—so often what feels like staticky interference, a kind of delayed or dispersed reaction to one's experiences in which it seems that one is somehow always slightly out of sync with oneself—not fully focused upon what one is hoping to see, nor completely attuned to what one is trying to hear—never quite where one wants to be, when one wants to be there. And, compounding the problem, to be present, one must somehow paradoxically remember being present, or anticipate being present, both of which, however, are not quite the same as being present.[30]

Trying to stay present is indeed difficult, and the act of describing events as they continue to unfold becomes more so. One of the challenges in continuing to write about my perceptual responses to the work is in trying to discern which events are the most meaningful to describe. It would be possible from here to focus mainly on those few events that are novel and new but I begin to doubt which events I am hearing for the first time. Similarly, the aforementioned multiperspectival view makes it difficult to know which past events to relate newer events to. My sense of memory is thrown into disarray; I am still trying to *just listen* but somehow the resignation into what would seem to be such a simple act still remains so difficult. It is the difficulty that comes from not understanding where I am in the music.

Gary Kose, commenting on Samuel Beckett's *Texts for Nothing* (1967), makes a similar remark, saying:

> A problem that emerges concerns transcendence and the difficulty of establishing a perspective. Being able to see clearly and to comprehend such things as setting and event, character and goals ... is for the narrators of the texts an inescapable plague. The effect is an illustration of the difficulty of beginning a narrative without perspective, which would ordinarily implicate a place, characters, events, and ending.[31]

Without a preordained sequential ordering, I must create my own narrative out of what is there. I perform the piece just as it performs upon me. Such long temporal spans influence my physical and mental condition. It inscribes in me its own sense of the past, its own history. I am reminded of the rather beautiful quote by Bergson, who said that "wherever anything lives, there is, open somewhere, a register in which time is being inscribed."[32] But knowing where that "somewhere" is over prolonged durations is so difficult; any sense of recollection is out of reach. The music continues to renew itself and I continue to live through it.

❋ ❋ ❋

In the following passage, forty-six and a half minutes into the track, the strings no longer play as a unit. Instead, their entries are staggered, with each note sounding as if it is gliding across the entry of the last. Given the relatively homophonic nature of the string writing up to now, this event feels significantly different. I am reminded once more of the physicality that is evoked from drawing the hair of the bow across the strings, although here it is not the collective sound of a string chord against the piano but individual string notes that are juxtaposed with each other. Against this, Feldman reintroduces a single repeated note on the piano. Here, these isolated pitches create a wholly different effect to when this kind of material last appeared in the piece, providing points of fixity or an anchor against the freer orientation of the strings. The spell is broken momentarily by a single piano chord leaping up to an isolated high note before the closely voiced gliding effect between the strings returns. I observe how the notes in the strings continually cross over, sometimes creating slight beating patterns as they conflict with the same pitch on the piano.

I am reminded of what a significant role registration plays in this piece. These chordal textures on the strings inhabit a narrow register and blend together. I find myself comparing this to the open, widely spaced piano chords that ensue and, in particular, to the two and a half octave arpeggio that has made its appearance once again. What registration helps support is the overall sense of distinction between the materials at play. At the same time, Feldman manipulates our ability to identify these materials through the use of octave transposition. Motifs sound distinct from one another, yet they are based on the same musical figure. At times, I am drawn to the content of the pitches, at other times register becomes the crucial element, providing marked territories in which materials open and close, blossom and retract.

Slightly later (fifty-three and a half minutes), an event takes place that is characteristic of other Feldman pieces from this period, which, to my knowledge, has not occurred up to now in this work: a rising chromatic figure, unaccompanied in the piano. As is typical of Feldman's approach when working with this kind of material, the pattern sounds almost even, but with certain durations subjected to a process of augmentation or diminution. Any semblance of evenness is obscured by this process, which results in what Feldman liked to refer to as "a crippled symmetry,"[33] an irregularity that disturbs the otherwise evenness and predictability of the pattern. In other pieces from this period such as Triadic Memories, these figures are often subjected to high levels of repetition, allowing the composer to present a series of near and exact repetitions in close succession. Here though, the figure sounds only once, and is followed by a new event: a broken chord. The rolling action of producing such a chord is unlike anything else that has occurred in the piece so far and, like the preceding chromatic figure, is registered as sounding significantly new.

Before I have chance to really respond to these newer events, Feldman reintroduces the chromatic figure again but this time on the strings as a variation on the original. As with the opening bars of the piece, I am reminded once again of the differences at play between the piano timbres and those of the strings, the onset of the piano notes with their stronger, transient attacks, compared to the softer entries of the strings and their abilities to sustain and control each note throughout its duration. Hearing these chromatic notes in succession on the strings affects its parametric attributes; on the piano I heard each note separately as a rising melody, but here the notes are built on top of one another, resulting in a closely voiced texture reminiscent of the "gliding" string section (forty-six and a half minutes).

What follows are further reminiscences; repetitions of repetitions, threads of memories, literal descriptions, comings and goings, changes of pace, orientations and disorientations. One senses that an ending might be on the horizon, somewhere, somehow, but there is nothing within the structure of the work to support this. This lack of teleology sets up its own conditions in which I experience time passing. It is not an absence of time that I witness, rather, I feel the weight of time bearing down on me at every instance. This *sense of time "bearing down on me" confronts me with my own condition of being. While, on the one hand, I feel acted upon by time itself, on the other I am reminded that time has no agency of its own.*

❋ ❋ ❋

The closing moments encapsulate the transient nature of this work. There is nothing to reach for and no immediate conclusions to draw from the seventy-six-minute duration. What I have witnessed and attempted to describe in the reflective commentary above has been brought about through the very act of listening and of living through Feldman's world of phenomenal transformations.

Notes

1   Morton Feldman, *Piano, Violin, Viola, Cello,* John Snijders, Josje Ter Haar, Ruben Sanderse, Job Ter Haar, Hat Hut Records HatART CD 6158, 1995, compact disc.

2   Morton Feldman, *Give My Regards to Eighth Street: Collected Writings of Morton Feldman*, ed. Bernard Harper Friedman (Boston, MA: Exact Change, 2000), 137.

3   Brian Kane, "Of Repetition, Habit and Involuntary Memory: An Analysis and Speculation Upon Morton Feldman's Final Composition," accessed November 19, 2017, http://www.cnvill.net/mfkane.pdf.

4   Bob Snyder, *Music and Memory: An Introduction* (Cambridge, MA: The MIT Press, 2000).

5   Tim Ingold, *Making: Anthropology, Archaeology, Art and Architecture* (Abingdon, Oxon: Routledge, 2013), xi.

6   Sebastian Claren, *Neither, Die Musik Morton Feldmans* (Hofheim: Wolke Verlag, 2000) as discussed in Kane, "Of Repetition," 1.

7   Jonathan Kramer, *The Time of Music* (New York: Schirmer Books, 1988), 61–62.

8   Tom Service, "A Guide to Morton Feldman's Music," *The Guardian*, November 12, 2012, https://www.theguardian.com/music/tomserviceblog/2012/nov/12/morton-feldman-contemporary-music-guide.

9   Kane, "Of Repetition," 1.

10 Dora A. Hanninen, "A Theory of Recontextualization in Music: Analyzing Phenomenal Transformations of Repetition," *Music Theory Spectrum* 25, no. 1 (March 2003): 59, https://doi.org/10.1525/mts.2003.25.1.59.

11 Morton Feldman, "Feldman-Lecture," July 2, 1987, quoted in Dora A. Hanninen, "Feldman, Analysis, Experience," *Twentieth-Century Music* 1, no. 2 (September 2004): 238, doi:10.1017/S1478572205000137.

12 Hanninen, "A Theory of Recontextualization," 61.

13 Steven Schick, *The Percussionist's Art: Same Bed Different Dreams* (Rochester: University of Rochester Press, 2006), 119–120.

14 Snyder, *Music and Memory*, 233–234.
15 Ibid., 66.
16 Morton Feldman, *Morton Feldman Essays*, ed. Walter Zimmermann (Kerpen: Beginner Press, 1985), 230.
17 Snyder, *Music and Memory*, 226.
18 Hanninen, "A Theory of Recontextualization," 61.
19 Kane, "Of Repetition," 27.
20 Feldman, *Morton Feldman Essays*, 124.
21 Catherine Laws, "Music and Language in the Work of Samuel Beckett" (D.Phil. diss., University of York, 1996), 211.
22 Snyder, *Music and Memory*, 99.
23 Feldman, *Morton Feldman Essays*.
24 Richard Glover and Bryn Harrison, *Overcoming Form: Reflections on Immersive Listening* (Huddersfield: University of Huddersfield Press, 2013), 48.
25 Tim Ingold, *Being Alive: Essays on Movement, Knowledge and Description* (London: Routledge, 2011), 9.
26 Tim Ingold, *Making: Anthropology, Archaeology, Art and Architecture* (London: Routledge, 2013), 20.
27 Penelope Reed Doob, *The Idea of the Labyrinth: From Classical Antiquity Through the Middle Ages* (Ithaca: Cornell University Press, 1994), 1.
28 Ingold, *Making*, 11.
29 Kane, "Of Repetition," 10.
30 Clark Lunberry, "*Remembrance of Things Present*: Steven Foster's *Repetition* Series Photographs, Morton Feldman's *Triadic Memories*," accessed November 19, 2017, http://www.cnvill.net/mflunberry.pdf, 2.
31 Gary Kose, "The Quest for Self-Identity: Time, Narrative, and the Late Prose of Samuel Beckett," *Journal of Constructivist Psychology* 15, no. 3 (2002): 177, http://dx.doi.org.libaccess.hud.ac.uk/10.1080/10720530290100415.
32 Henri Bergson, *Creative Evolution* (New York: Henry Holt, 1911), 16.
33 Morton Feldman, "Crippled Symmetry" (1981), in *Give My Regards to Eighth Street: Collected Writings of Morton Feldman*, ed. Bernard Harper Friedman (Cambridge, MA: Exact Change, 2000), 134–149.

Postlude to Chapter One

Richard Glover

To listen through *Piano, Violin, Viola, Cello* is to experience multiple forms of disorientation and dislocation. Jennie and I both discussed the fragmented, alternating form which is continually being broken up throughout the piece, and Bryn describes how he is storing information in an "incomplete form," which we both experienced: the listening experience never felt fully formed, or finalized—there were only ever patches, shards, producing what Bryn describes as "both familiarity and confusion." This clarity in one's own disorientation, through a sense of simultaneously knowing and bewilderment, was felt keenly by both Jennie and I, aligning closely with Bryn's observations.

We noted the emergent similarities between this experience of the Feldman, and the structuring of Bryn's chapter; the fragmented nature of the writing—caused by interspersing with personal reflections from the listening, and numerous quotes—mirrored the listening experience. There was a sense that Bryn's writing adopted a diary form, and we as the readers were being led through his experience of the piece, as it happened.

We explored Bryn's comment on how the perception of materials was entirely dependent on all others that have preceded them; Feldman seems to shape our memories, not in a controlling manner but rather a sense of nudging, or prompting. There is a strong sense that Feldman's structural decisions are indenting upon each new perception from the piece.

Bryn's comments upon Feldman's repetition are particularly appropriate in discussing the two levels of repetition Feldman employs—both the larger structural phrases or blocks and the micro-level repetition of single units of material. In *Piano, Violin, Viola, Cello*, the continual reintroduction of phrases that "differ in character" serve to "manipulate the listener's perspective"; Bryn discusses how the present is reinforced through these different levels of repetition, erasing preceding events. Both Jennie and I explored the notion of this structural approach as feeling like a *test*: Of what is my memory capable? What can it withstand? I didn't hear memories being erased as such, but rather I felt that my memories were being challenged. At certain points, I would ask myself whether what I am hearing is the same information as what I have heard before—and does that matter? Being able to make these comparisons, or connections, becomes considerably difficult; at a certain point in listening, I realize I am not capable, and I seem to consciously yield to this. Jennie and I both felt that, as the piece continued on, it became less and less important to retain this focus on exact similarity in recollection; Bryn's maze is changing its design continually, to the point of impossibility of recollection. While we were directed toward considerations of repetition, comparability, we never experienced a sense of regularity, and thus searching for repetition becomes unnecessary.

Jennie stated that part of her enjoyment of the listening experience of the piece is its success of breaking a temporal grid. She learned to listen more for irregularity than regularity, and found the absence of a grid to be the most reliable thing. That absence itself becomes the stability; perhaps this is akin to the reinforcement of the present—erasure of memory—which Bryn discusses. Jennie sensed a beauty in the shared breathing between the instrumentalists; she described what she heard as living "organisms" that the four instruments together have created between them, through the detail and performativity in the sound. She felt she was breathing with these organisms and aligned herself with specific patterns and motions despite—or rather because of—their irregularity. Their "organicism" is more appealing, more inherently approachable, than any kind of strict pulse would be. She states how a regularly ticking pulse, or an adherence to a single texture for any appreciable length of time, would be the greatest possible aberration; the reliability of *irregularity* is what sustains her throughout the listening experience.

Considering again the notion of the piece as a test, or challenge, Bryn notes how the piece brings an awareness of the "limitations of my understanding and, ultimately, of my own sense of being." Jennie stated her memory had been "toyed with"—a phrase here or there was a decoy, deliberately designed to mislead. At some point toward the end of the piece, I experienced a strong sense of "do not try" as if in response to "what can I recall?" being asked by the structural design of the piece itself; the task of remembering, sifting through, was monumentally impossible for me.

Bryn was encouraged to "stop making sense of things," as with the aforementioned "yielding"; Jennie focused upon how her degree of *tracking* as a listener would occasionally gain emphasis over a simpler attention, before ebbing away again. How much does our zoom level transform? How can we gain a sense of scale over this piece, during the experience of listening? Bryn describes material being simultaneously "out-of-reach" and "close-at-hand"—attempting to find a middle-distance experiential position is futile, as the repetition of material seems to continually pull him between different levels of listening focus.

While these experiences may seem to be phrased negatively, Jennie and I discussed how there is a vast range of shades of different instrumental colors (the instrumental texture is fragile, on the edge of a precipice, yet there is no sense of a jarring quality to what is heard), but much of that vastness is actually superimposed by our own memories; the misrecollections, disorientation caused by similar phrases and units of material, actually seem to engender different colors and different tactile qualities each new time we think we hear something similar. Jennie noticed how the surface of the piece is so different from the way it works, and I'd suggest further the way that we work, or act, upon it. The knowledge that our own cognitive processes are "filling in" these materials with nuanced color, the timbral changes, seems like a particularly powerful concept. Similarly, but perhaps more pragmatically, Jennie moved into various different spaces in the room in which she listened to the piece, as a strategy to deal with the slight differences in material; by taking subjective control over her own listening experience, she developed an approach to navigating through the tangled web of repetitions and near-repetitions Feldman deploys. Bryn describes the listening as a "lived experience," and these two notions of subjective shading and objective listening position expand out this notion.

Bryn mentions Sebastian Claren's reference to the monolithic nature of a piece such as *Piano, Violin, Viola, Cello*, but it is quite a different sense to that of the Spiegel and Möller monolithic of Jennie's chapter. This piece feels *exponential*: we start with two things, which are then multiplied by everything else, and this structured constellation continues continuing; it is not a flat, open expanse, but a highly detailed network that is actively expanding. Jennie suggests that perhaps the instrumentalists would not be able to achieve this openness to time unfolding in a smaller timespan, and I am again reminded of the concept of duration as a compositional *tool*, in which transformations in listeners' experiences can be brought about by careful approaches to extended durations.

I focused upon Bryn's notion that *Piano, Violin, Viola, Cello* offers "no opportunity to reflect," which I experienced particularly through what emerged as the middle third or so of the piece. There is a quiet insistence through the materials, always transforming, and attempting to coerce me into comparing and searching for patterns; it feels like there is no letup. I wrote about the lack of reflective opportunity in my chapter on Ikeda's + tracks, but this is a wholly separate kind of nonreflective environment. There is space, silence, moderation here—yet there is a continual disorientation, a nagging sense of one's own limitations of understanding, which affords an entirely unique temporal experience to emerge.

CHAPTER TWO

Musical Brevity in James Saunders' *Compatibility hides itself* and *511 possible mosaics*

Bryn Harrison

Having put to rest the research I had undertaken for my previous chapter on Morton Feldman's 76-minute *Piano, Violin, Viola, Cello* (1987), I began to wonder about works at the opposite end of the spectrum: those of extremely short duration. The early pieces of James Saunders came to mind immediately. I have known James since my mid-twenties and I attended the premiere performances of several of his very short works between 1997 and 2000. I remember distinctly, during a concert given at the Ryedale Festival in North Yorkshire, England, during the summer of 1997, hearing for the first time a collection of pieces entitled *Separated we shall be for ever my friends, like the wild geese lost in the clouds* (1997). The shortest of these lasted maybe only three or four seconds and the longest less than twenty. I recall the ensuing sense of bemusement from many of the audience members present that evening; each piece seemed to have ended before it had really begun.

Over time—between 1997 and 2000—I equipped myself with the skills necessary to listen to these pieces more attentively and, in the process, developed a growing appreciation of them. However, by the start of the new millennium, Saunders had abandoned shorter pieces in favor of a new, long-term project entitled *#[unassigned]*. This allowed him to write longer works by combining the types of materials that might be found in the previous short pieces into larger modular structures. With the advent of this new project came the end of a relatively intensive period of writing almost exclusively short works. While #*[unassigned]* might be considered the project in which the potentials of these early compositional approaches came to maturation, it is the short pieces written prior to #*[unassigned]* that I will be addressing here. Although these pieces belong to an early period of Saunders' output and reflect a time when the composer was still developing his compositional thinking, I argue that they remain worthy of investigation on account of their radical approach to dealing with temporality and the perceptual questions that they raise for the listener. These early pieces are documented in Saunders' PhD thesis, "Developing a Modular Approach to Music" (University of Huddersfield, 2003).

In this chapter I will examine different performed versions of Saunders' pieces *Compatibility hides itself* (1998–99) and *511 possible mosaics* (1999) and discuss their temporal effect on me as a listener. Although the durations of these works are dramatically different to the Feldman piece considered in the previous chapter, when researching and listening to Saunders' pieces I found myself contemplating similar issues, most notably the way in which memory comes into play. As in the Feldman, the element of scale leads me to questions about the thresholds of perceptibility. Saunders examines these limits through a series of works that, taken as single entities, deny memory rehearsal due to their brevity, whereas in the Feldman my apprehension of the work is tested through an enforced disorientation of memory that takes place over a large durational span.

At the time when these short pieces were being written (1996–2000), Saunders was considering how musical materials might operate outside of the formal constraints of the twelve-minute chamber work or the twenty-minute orchestral piece.[1] He contends that "[e]xtreme durations challenge assumptions. They question how we compose, perform and experience music, as well as the cultural institutions that mediate this experience."[2] In writing his short works, Saunders was not only making a musical statement, but also taking a political stance. His approach problematized the usual limits of convention, empowering him to ask: What if a piece was only a few seconds long? What kinds of materials could constitute such a piece and how would they be presented? How might working with such short durations affect our understanding of musical time and how might memory operate in this context? How could individual parts to such pieces be combined and organized? How might these works be programmed and disseminated? As well as providing some immediate answers to these questions, each of Saunders' short pieces opens up lines of inquiry that he continued to investigate in his later music. Each piece is an experiment in which Saunders sets out to discover the full potential of short-duration works.

My decisions regarding which recorded performances of Saunders' pieces I would discuss in this chapter were colored by personal preference, but also influenced by the practical issues associated with which recordings were available to me. I found two versions of *Compatibility hides itself* performed by Annie Parker (flute), Brian Lee (violin), and Tim Parkinson (piano) particularly compelling and, during my search for other potential recordings, was sent a collection of sixty-three versions of *511 possible mosaics* performed in a single concert in 2013 by ensemble 175 East, which I found to be a fascinating vehicle for discussing multiple perspectives on a single short work. These two choices therefore offer slightly differing perspectives on Saunders' output from this period.

Compatibility hides itself

This piece is written for any possible instrumental combination from a choice of parts written for flute, alto flute, clarinet, bass clarinet, horn, trumpet, trombone, percussion, vibraphone, harp, piano, violin, cello, and double bass. The score comprises individual pages of parts without specific instruction as to how these might be combined or aligned. Although, theoretically, any part may be combined with any other, these parts were created initially for specific instrumental combinations and written for particular concert situations. For example, for the first performance, the piece was designed in a duo version for Annie Parker (flute) and Tim Parkinson (piano), but later versions were made for other ensembles, such as the trumpet and percussion version created for Duo Contour.

The title for this piece comes from a quotation by John Cage:

Sometimes compatibility hides itself. Probably, we are ultimately compatible with everything, but we make it impossible for things to reach us, or they just don't cross our paths, or some such thing.[3]

The underlying suggestion is that states of unpredictability and surprise emerge from situations in which sounds come together in unexpected or unintended ways. Saunders expressed to me elsewhere that he was also concerned about the arbitrary nature of his decision-making; "Why put these materials together in this one way? What about all the possibilities these decisions prevent?"[4]

Saunders writes of *Compatibility hides itself*:

In the piece, the separate instrumental parts are precisely notated but can be played together as the performers wish, enabling the possibility of unforeseen coincidences to appear in the music … the amount of overlap between parts, if any, is up to the performers.[5]

Each instrumental part "lasts between 11–14 seconds, contains three to six short gestures (sometimes a gesture is a single sound) and normally has a sense of closure."[6] The overall duration of the piece depends upon when the players choose to start in relation to the others. In theory, it is permissible for a player to begin after other players have ended but, in practice, the materials lend themselves to certain levels of interaction. Throughout all five of the audio recordings made available to me, the instrumental lines overlap, which results in durations that vary from thirteen to thirty seconds.

It is the nature of the overlap between instruments and the textural interplay created from these interactions that I find particularly fascinating. In each instance I hear the same material, but the overall degrees of elongation and contraction that result from the various ways in which the parts are juxtaposed lead me to contrasting temporal experiences. Some versions result in denser textures, while others appear more sparse.

The reflective commentary below compares two versions of this piece, both performed by a trio of flute, violin, and piano, each of which demonstrates differing degrees of interaction. These two versions were performed by the same trio—Parker, Parkinson, and Lee—during the same concert. Performances would occur in different halves of the programme, or with other pieces programmed in between. Separating two versions in concert proved to be an effective way of giving the audience time to adjust and reflect on the first version, and to be prepared more fully for the second realization. The short account of this work will provide the necessary contextual underpinning for the more in-depth discussion of a greater number of versions of the *511 possible mosaics* that follows later in the chapter.

Notes taken while listening to Version 1 of Compatibility hides itself

The piece slips by almost unnoticed.
I am left with an impression of this brief piece, but can recall few of the details.
The textural surface sounds "pointillistic" and the language gestural, comprising short groups of notes displaced over different octaves.
Each part sounds carefully structured, intervallically coherent, and rhythmically organized.
The fact that the flute leads in this particular version seemed significant in forcing me to hear the entries of the violin and piano in immediate profile to the first entry.
Very quickly though, the lines became intertwined, making distinctions between instruments difficult.
Following a final isolated gesture from the piano, the piece is over.

Commentary on notes taken to Version 1

My notes convey the initial difficulty I had in coming to terms with the brevity of the music. I felt frustrated by the limits of my understanding, by how little I could comprehend in a single take, and by the scant notes I was able to make. Just as it had when I first heard these pieces in concert some twenty years previously, the piece confounded my expectations; a level of unfamiliarity had set in once again as I had forgotten the demands that this kind of music placed upon me as a listener. I was left with the absence of the piece so soon after having acknowledged its presence. All I had to show for the experience was an afterthought—a memory or trace—that eluded direct recollection.

What was in this trace? In the above notes I mentioned the significance of the gestural aspect of the language. I was also able to identify similarities in intervallic content and a sense of unity within this single listen despite my inability to confidently attribute note groupings to particular instruments. It was perhaps inevitable that, in the densest of moments, making an immediate perceptual association between line and instrument would be difficult over such a short time span. Over a longer duration it may have been possible for me to identify each instrumental line more readily and follow each strand but here, over such a short duration, I found identifying melodic phrases of similar register, dynamics, articulation, and pitch content particularly difficult. What I was left with was a sense of intervallic and gestural recognition taking precedence over the identification of individual instrumental lines.

Notes taken on listening to Version 2

The violin starts with the piano entering some two or three seconds later.
The entry of the flute is staggered by roughly the same duration, overlapping slightly with the piano's second phrase.
The instrumental parts are staggered to a greater degree than the first version, resulting in an elongation of the overall duration of events.
The texture sounds more "porous."
As a result of this stretching of parts, the flute ends much later (relatively speaking) than the other two instruments, creating the impression of a tapering off in time, a final thread spinning out of a tightly constructed network.
The delayed entry of each instrument creates a thinner texture and thus makes the identification of each line more clearly perceptible.
In particular, the opening violin gesture and the closing flute gesture stand apart, taking on their own identities.
Silences emerge out of activity.

Most noticeably, a kind of dialectic is established whereby the parts appear to "talk to" one another rather than "talking over" one another.

Commentary on notes to Version 2

Immediately, I see that vast differences exist between my perceptions of Version 1 and Version 2. While the instrumental parts themselves remain unchanged from Version 1 to Version 2, the ways in which they are juxtaposed against, and consequently "behave" with one another, is considerably different. The entries are staggered to a far greater degree in Version 2, allowing for the possibility of a gesture to sound after a previous gesture in another part has ended. When this occurs, I hear the second phrase as a consequence to the first, creating a strong dialectical relationship between them. There is more of a sense of horizontality here—I hear each line as a distinct entity—and I am able to perceive the details of the instrumental writing more readily.

Remarks following further listenings

Returning to Version 1 immediately after listening to Version 2 was a particularly revealing exercise. The higher level of textural density in Version 1 produced a greater sense of contained energy and the illusion of a faster tempo. The overall structure felt more compact as each part seemingly competed for its own space. Phrases had immediacy and urgency of the kind that was absent in Version 2. It was as if, faced with the challenge of performing music of such brevity, every note counted for so much, leading to a situation in which the performance space became focused and charged. Returning to Version 2 again for comparison, I was struck by the relatively relaxed pace of the music and a pronounced sense of having "slowed down." There was no sense of competing for space, and phrases had the opportunity to breathe.

 I isolated the two versions and listened to each of them again, between ten and twenty times, often pausing to make notes in the process. With each hearing the details of each instrumental line became more apparent. I discovered an abundance of nuance, particularly with regard to dynamics and articulation. Some notes were slurred while others sounded staccato. Those phrases that ended in a longer-held note would seem to project forward in time, while those ending in a staccato felt more arrested. Often these different types of gesture would be overlaid, providing fluctuating levels of micro-activity. Where lines became juxtaposed, notes in the same register were masked, and this led to greater degrees of textural ambiguity. The brevity of each version meant that I could anticipate entries with some precision. Over time, familiarity highlighted the differences I observed between these versions.

511 possible mosaics

Compatibility hides itself highlighted for Saunders the advantages of repeated hearings and suggested ways this idea might be developed further. Saunders writes in his thesis, "I like the idea of needing to return to music, and with that return having a different experience of it."[7] *511 possible mosaics* can be seen as the outworking of this idea. The piece was written for the New Zealand ensemble 175 East and is scored for the nine core members of the group. The "mosaic" in the title relates to the small fragments of sound that make up each part: small note groupings that might be combined to form larger collective structures. The piece is entirely modular in its construction; the different parts may be performed individually or in combination from two to nine players but, unlike *Compatibility hides itself*, exact synchronization of parts is required. As the title suggests, there are 511 possible combinations from the pool of nine instrumental parts.[8]

Every version is created by superimposing time points and assigning certain pitches to each layer. However, each part is distinct, and there are clear perceivable differences between each version. Saunders discusses this further when he says:

> I wanted the piece to be able to reveal different facets of itself on separate hearings, to provide a different perspective, opening windows on parts of the texture that might be more deeply hidden in other versions. Some passages are hidden in certain combinations, but revealed in others, and in the fuller versions in particular a lot is covered. Only by hearing different versions can more be learnt about the piece.[9]

These facets and the ways in which each hearing offers a different perspective on the work are discussed in the commentary below. These notes are based on close listening to a recording made by Radio New Zealand of a concert given by 175 East in 2013. One of the advantages of this piece is that it can be adapted to fit with those instruments available. The instrumentation for this particular concert consisted of flute, clarinet, bass clarinet, bass trombone, percussion, and double bass. Artistic director Samuel Holloway had the inspired idea of presenting all the possible versions available for that particular instrumentation, from solo versions right up to the version for all six players. From the pool of six instrumentalists, there are a total of sixty-three possible versions. As Saunders has pointed out, each version provides a unique listening experience and a different perspective on the materials.

Listening to the concert version of 511 *possible mosaics*

The following account is of all sixty-three versions performed in immediate succession, amounting to a total duration of twenty-two minutes. These versions represent all possible combinations for that sextet, including the six solos and the version for the full sextet. Each of the sixty-three versions is performed once only, meaning that the instrumentation is always changing. The sequence in which these are performed appears to be entirely arbitrary.

In recording the following observations, my initial intention was to comment on most, but not necessarily all, of the versions. I had imagined that certain versions would get clumped together as I began to fatigue and build up more of a general impression of the piece. However, on close listening I found I was able to write on each, although in some instances my comments were fairly scant. I began by simply listening to the whole event through, while marking time stamps against the relative start times of each version. Then, I went back and listened to the whole event again, making notes on my perceptual responses as I did so. It was often necessary to pause the recording after a particular version, either for reflection or to allow myself the physical time needed to make notes. I changed few of these comments subsequently, but reworded some of my descriptions in the interest of clarity.

Notes taken while listening

0:00 *511 possible mosaics [#046]* flute, clarinet, and bass clarinet

The combination of flute, clarinet, and bass clarinet reveals different articulations, particularly on the flute—breathy sounds, staccatos, tremolandos.
Distinct note groupings occur in each part, making it difficult not to hear these as phrases.
Articulations appear incidentally through the texture while others get masked.
Each instrument occupies its own range, leading to a sense of balance and of perceptual clarity.
Overlapping phrases played on different instruments get chunked together, leading to nested groupings of localized activity.
Silence is important—I move from one localized event to the next.
Time becomes spatialized.
Phrases jostle for space and overlap in unpredictable ways.

0:23 *[#075]* flute, bass clarinet, and bass trombone

The distinct timbral difference of the muted bass trombone provides immediate contrast to the preceding version.

The muted to open notes in the bass trombone part reveal transitions through time (particularly the final note), and I am reminded of the fact that sounds that are timbrally transformative contain a greater sense of motion.
I am aware of the final note of the bass trombone pushing forward at the end, which provides more of a sense of finality than in the previous version.

0:45 [#024] clarinet and double bass

The reduction from three parts to two is immediately noticeable.
This does not appear to result in a perceptual increase in clock time but a distinct lessening in the amount of information to process is evident.

1:11 [#026] bass clarinet and bass trombone

Having heard these parts together less than a minute earlier, their context is changed; the absence of the flute places emphasis on the resultant lower register band.
The two parts complement each other, creating a homogenous texture.
The overall passing of events feels smoother and more linear.
Notes emerge and recede through the overall duration of the event.
Both instruments end on a crescendo leading to a stronger sense of closure.

1:34 [#131] flute, clarinet, bass clarinet, and bass trombone

I recognize the repeating material from the version above but the bass clarinet and bass trombone parts sound changed by the addition of the flute. Even the interactions between them feel different.
I realize that I have already heard all of the above lines during the preceding one and a half minutes but fail to hear them in the same way; I am forced to group overlapping phrases together. Each resultant temporal gestalt takes on its own unrepeatable characteristics.

1:58 [#030] bass clarinet and double bass

The reduction to two instruments provides considerably more space.
I anticipate the ending some two-thirds of the way through.
More endings—long held notes that are pronounced.

2:23 [#002] solo clarinet

The arrival of the first solo piece feels particularly significant: no interactions, no dialogue.
Although I have heard this part three times previously, I hear this material anew.
The isolated event feels somehow longer in time.
Each "mosaic" is highly definable—a distinct "pattern," a perceptual unit.
I am carried forward from one to the next.
Each moment of silence provides an anticipation toward the next note grouping.

2:46 [#162] flute, bass clarinet, percussion, and double bass

The first entry of the percussion feels significant.
The nonpitched profile dominates somewhat, masking other parts and producing what feels like gravitational pulls downward that seem counterintuitive to the implied goal-directedness of the flute, bass clarinet, and double bass parts.

3:08 [#144] flute, clarinet, bass trombone, and double bass

Most of the gaps get filled in, resulting in very little silence. This provides a greater sense of continuity but perhaps a lessening of anticipation. I do not have time to anticipate the arrival of the next phrase but simply listen to the busy stream of interactions.
There is a far greater level of timbral interplay in this version.

3:31 [#141] flute, clarinet, bass trombone, and percussion

A series of stilted progressions.
Much more of a sense of space (perhaps as a result of the closing off of silences in the previous version).
I clump events together and move from one chunking of activity to the next. The chunking is far from predictable—each version is unique in its divisions and sense of interactions.
Building up a perceptual "map" of events and potential interactions seems impossible.

3:51 [#261] flute, clarinet, bass clarinet, bass trombone, and percussion

I begin to anticipate when each new version will begin.
Each feels somehow predictable and yet unique.
Like a fired Raku pot, the form that each takes remains the same but the details are always different.

4:12 [#070] flute, percussion, and double bass

Instrumental changes are more acute, resulting in less homogeneity.
Distinct timbral and registral differences allow me to separate out my listening between instruments.
This takes me away from the processual aspect of the work and toward the individual parts.
As a result I am less concerned with time passing.

4:33 [#020] clarinet and bass trombone

Sense of dialogue between instruments.
This conversation creates continuity.

4:54 [#075] clarinet, bass clarinet, and bass trombone

It is becoming difficult to be sure that I am hearing a particular version for the first time.

There is a certain confusion of the senses.
Parts feel familiar and yet it is only the endings that I am able to predict.
I develop a strong sense of being carried along and, in the process, submitting to the seemingly random ordering of events.

5:14 *[#054]* flute, bass clarinet, bass trombone, and double bass

Again, the interactions feel familiar and yet each version exists as a complete entity—like snowflakes.
I do not at any point hear each version as part of a continuum—each plays itself out in its own unique way and yet I can no longer say what makes every version distinct from every other.

5:36 *[#018]* clarinet and bass clarinet

The interactions feel stronger, almost preconceived. To what extent is this the result of the instruments belonging to the same family?
Notes clump together to form their own unique groupings.
I am taken from one grouping to the next.

5:58 *[#011]* flute and bass clarinet

I feel as if I am privy to another chance conversation between two instruments.
I feel the urge to hear all the possible duo versions.
Different chunking to the last, again unpredictable.

6:18 *[#005]* solo bass trombone

Another solo version and again a space opens up.
I am less concerned about time passing—phrases feel as if they can breathe.
I begin to consider more the effect that the levels of interaction between instruments has on my sense of time passing; to what degree does synchronicity affect my listening?

6:40 *[#100]* bass clarinet, bass trombone, and percussion

Bit by bit, successive elements of the "inner-components" are revealed.
Simultaneously, newer and newer versions blur my understanding.

7:01 *[#135]* flute, clarinet, bass clarinet, and double bass

Notes merge, filling the timespan.
Instruments jostle for space.
I wrestle with the larger registral palette—notes jump out across several octaves.

7:20 *[#079]* clarinet, bass clarinet, and double bass

Clarinet and bass clarinet blend into one homogenous sound, pitted against the double bass.

7:40 *[#001]* solo flute

Sudden exposure of a solo version is revealing, this being the second.
Again, the absence of interaction with another instrumental part is registered with particular significance.
Highly gestural with disjunct motion.
Plosives—series of consonants the mouth shapes provides changes of articulation.
Different modes of articulation (staccato notes, breathy sounds) are clearly present as are the subtle distinctions in duration between individual notes.
Note groupings appear to have a sense of closure, particularly at the end where I observe a resolutely final note in the lower register.
Phrases feel balanced, leading me from one note grouping to the next.
I am carried along by these phrases without any immediate concern for the brevity of the music.

8:01 *[#197]* clarinet, bass clarinet, percussion, and double bass

The contrast to the previous version is enormous.
I begin to feel that each is defined more in terms of its general timbral and registral characteristics than by their harmonic or rhythmic profile.
I am aware of the weight of the lower voices.
More arrested than projected.

8:22 *[#267]* flute, clarinet, bass clarinet, percussion, and double bass

The time frame becomes filled out again.
A mass of sound of changing density.
Lots of timbral ambiguity through the merging of lines.
The thinning of texture toward the end becomes a goal-defining feature.

8:42 *[#103]* bass clarinet, bass trombone, and double bass

Lower register versions are generally less distinguishable from one another but the start feels noticeably slower and the ending has a strong sense of closure.

9:03 *[#085]* clarinet, bass trombone, and percussion

Clearer divisions in the overall texture here.
Slices of sound.
Stronger onsets to notes create clearer structural divisions.
I am unable to anticipate when these will occur.

9:25 *[#052]* flute, clarinet, and double bass

Clear sense of line and structural division.
Versions that combine higher instruments (flute and clarinet) with a single lower instrument provide particular registral points of interest.

9:47 *[#055]* flute, bass clarinet, and percussion

This version almost sounds like a variation on the last.
It is becoming increasingly difficult to focus in on the individual identity of each version as concentration becomes an issue.

10:07 *[#058]* flute, bass clarinet, and double bass

Pizzicato in the double bass provides points of focus.
To what extent am I still able to focus in the moment?
So many anticipations—I anticipate endings and then beginnings.
I can navigate my way through the structure without being aware of the details.

10:27 *[#003]* solo bass clarinet

My attention is restored.
I focus on the intervallic leaps and the quick changes in articulation.
The moment opens up, drawing me in.

10:46 *[#303]* flute, bass clarinet, bass trombone, percussion, and double bass

The contrast to the last is enormous.
I am aware of the bass clarinet being present but somehow buried in the texture.

11:06 *[#178]* flute, bass trombone, percussion, and double bass

There seems to be a moment some two-thirds of the way through the denser versions in which I anticipate the ending, which then seems to stretch on just a little longer than I expected.

11:26 *[#014]* flute and percussion

This version has seemingly unique characteristics. The transient qualities of the two floor toms and the sharp onset of the flute notes result in a dynamic interplay.
A rhythmic profile is more evident than in other versions, leading to a succession of interactions that is markedly different from the textural continuity of the last.

11:46 *[#147]* flute, clarinet, percussion, and double bass

As with the previous version, the space feels charged and alive but the addition of clarinet and double bass creates a heightened sense of textural interplay.

12:07 *[#009]* solo double bass

So many of the details hidden in the previous versions now come to the fore.
Every note seems to require a new articulation.
The physicality of performance carries me forward from one phrase to the next.

12:27 *[#036]* bass trombone and percussion

Echoes of the flute and percussion version prevail.
Again, a sense of dynamic interplay, but operating within a similar low register.

12:47 *[#394]* flute, clarinet, bass clarinet, bass trombone, percussion, and double bass

The only version in which all six instruments are present.
Gradual intensification of activity.
Once all the instruments are at play (which occurs within the first few seconds) there is a relatively distributed degree of activity between parts but with noticeable thinning and thickening of texture.
What I hear is a chunking of materials—these "nested" activities promote a sense of interaction.
All the spaces are completely filled—I am consequently more drawn to the textural mass than the articulations within it.
Unfolding successions of events become blanketed yet they are still carried forward and anticipate a strong sense of closure.
Time becomes a single span—one continuum (with swells and contours present within) rather than as a series of articulations that make up a collective span.
Is time still as directional? Does it take up the same amount of perceived clock time?
Do the perceptual boundaries only lie at the start and the end?

13:08 *[#132]* flute, clarinet, bass clarinet, and percussion

The omission of two instruments from the previous version creates a sense of contrast, particularly through the absence of the double bass, which tends to fill out the texture.
More chunking of note groupings.

13:28 *[#039]* bass trombone and double bass

The particular instrumental combination leads to smoother transitions and a greater sense of continuity.

13:49 *[#042]* percussion and double bass

Not surprisingly, the percussion part provides an entirely different interaction with the double bass than the last.
The overall motion has less of a sense of perceptual continuity.

14:09 *[#213]* clarinet, bass trombone, percussion, and double bass

Constant peaks of activity—each instrument has its own features which push through the texture, rupturing its surface: a slap note on the clarinet, a crescendo trombone note that changes from a closed to open mute position, an accented floor tom, an accented pizzicato on the double bass.

14:30 *[#106]* bass clarinet, percussion, and double bass

All instruments in same lower register.
Lack of definition—bass clarinet and double bass follow a general contour.
Articulations are present, especially in the bass clarinet and double bass parts but are difficult at times to identify.
Rhythms feel less irregular and unpredictable.
I move from one chunked event to the next.

14:50 *[#191]* clarinet, bass clarinet, bass trombone, and percussion

Instrumentation provides smoother transitions through the time envelope and a greater sense of continuity.

15:10 *[#027]* bass clarinet and percussion

Sense of excavation—the removal of parts (clarinet and bass trombone) unearths others.
A greater feeling of space but resonance from the floor toms "fills in the gaps" and provides a sense of transition and continuity.

15:30 *[#064]* flute, bass trombone, and percussion

Interesting groupings of events occur.
Greater sense of separation between collective events.
Time seems to move in blocks from one of these events to the next.

15:54 *[#156]* flute, bass clarinet, bass trombone, and percussion

Piece seems to move quicker as events become more cumulative but does not seem to overtly affect my overall sense of the version being shorter.

16:15 *[#067]* flute, bass trombone, and double bass

Time seems to pass more smoothly here.
Ending feels pronounced.
I cannot help anticipating these endings. Even within such a short time span I shift my attention toward the approaching ending some two-thirds of the way through.

16:36 *[#338]* clarinet, bass clarinet, bass trombone, percussion, and double bass

Higher level of activity.
Sudden interactions.

16:57 *[#010]* flute and clarinet

A series of (dialogic) utterances, sometimes conveyed simultaneously.
Again, the end feels particularly noticeable—almost a place where the instrumentalists compete for space.

Timbre plays such an integral role in creating degrees of separation between parts.
Strong sense of closure but the ending was slightly unexpected.

17:16 [#091] clarinet, percussion, and double bass

Clumping of activity but floor toms and double bass fill out the resonance space. Ending once again feels slightly unexpected as only the double bass has a crescendo.

17:36 [#048] flute, clarinet, and bass trombone

Each entry is with a single note.
Very quickly the texture becomes highly active.
I try to take in the details but it is difficult.
I find myself able to identify individual lines with a little more clarity but their ever-changing contexts make the identification of detail so difficult.

17:56 [#017] flute and double bass

The overall texture sounds surprisingly filled out and yet the registral distinctions allow me to shift my attention readily between the two parts. Less homogeneity supports the sense of music in two parts.

18:17 [#122] bass trombone, percussion, and double bass

My attention is drawn from one instrument to the next—the percussion, the bass trombone, and, eventually, in the very final moments, to the double bass.
It is as if the double bass, which sounds so foregrounded in other versions, is buried beneath the other parts, only to be excavated at the end.

18:38 [#194] clarinet, bass clarinet, bass trombone, and double bass

I begin by listening to the overall texture but move my attention to the activity between the clarinet and bass clarinet.
I register that I have heard these two instruments play their duo before (5:36) but it was too long ago for me to recall what was similar or different to what I was listening to just now.

19:00 [#021] clarinet and percussion

Any sense of linearity is replaced by a series of abrupt stops and starts. It is evident from any of the previous versions that harmonic consistency contributes greatly to a sense of motion and carries the music forward in time.

19:20 [#049] flute, clarinet, and percussion

The floor toms almost appear to accentuate the activities in the flute and clarinet parts.

Again, a sense of stops and starts but, with the addition of the flute, the event becomes transformed into a contrapuntal tapestry.

19:41 [#233] bass clarinet, bass trombone, percussion, and double bass

The surface is constantly shifting.
A myriad of activity—a mosaic.
It is so difficult to get a hold on these versions which pull in so many directions at once.

20:01 [#088] clarinet, bass trombone, and double bass

All the low instruments present at once.
It is difficult to discern details in these versions as events become so homogenized.

20:22 [#013] flute and bass trombone

Articulations on each instrument are clearly audible due to the differences in instrumental range.
Parts seem to play off one another, occasionally reaching points of near-synchronization.

20:43 [#264] flute, clarinet, bass clarinet, bass trombone, and double bass

High level of activity, filling out the space.
Dense and textural.
I listen through but miss most of the detail.

21:03 [#283] flute, clarinet, bass trombone, percussion, and double bass

The inclusion of percussion creates points of delineation.
Somehow less active than the previous version, despite having the same number of players.

21:23 [#006] solo percussion

The inclusion of this solo version so late in the sequence of events comes as a surprise.
This version has less of a sense of anticipation and I find myself concentrating on each moment and being less concerned for the overall teleology of the work.

21:42 [#076] clarinet, bass clarinet, and percussion

The final version reveals a strong sense of interaction between the clarinet and bass clarinet.
As with the flute, clarinet, and percussion version, the floor toms appear to accentuate the activities in the other parts.
I continue to play out more imaginary versions in my head, which are as unspecific and unpredictable as the versions I have just listened to.

Commentary on listening through the sixty-three versions

Concentrating on this marathon event proved to be no easy task. However, I was surprised to find that in each case the introduction of a new version would "cleanse the palette" and allow me to hear the piece afresh. Each part's characteristics and specific note placements meant that the novelty of hearing one version after another never quite wore off. Each version would reveal new synchronicities through which phrases would appear to play off one another or merge into a series of successive events. In certain cases, an instrument would appear "excavated" from the ruinous mass of the preceding version. At other times, a part would become subsumed or buried within the densely layered texture of the piece.

Through this process, each line was set in a different light to the last. Instrumental parts became recontextualized, often to the extent that they sounded, to my ears, like entirely new parts. At times, delicate duos and trios emerged from the denser homogenous mass revealing characterful interactions. The sudden arrival of a solo version would provide a welcome contrast to the preceding events. Details would reveal themselves and the overall shape and contour of the line would become apparent. I found it difficult to hear each note separately rather than as part of a phrase. Inevitably, notes in close proximity would form their own groupings and be heard as phrases. As with *Compatibility hides itself*, where note groupings in different instrumental parts overlap, additional groupings would be created. While the relative degrees of continuity/discontinuity would reveal different aspects of temporal succession, the thinning of the texture toward the end became a goal-defining feature. As I found myself commenting on more than one occasion, when the temporal framework became "filled out" with notes, I would quickly begin to anticipate the endings.

In her study of musical time, Barbara R. Barry notes that an increase in information density tends to lead to the perception of a longer time period, since it takes a greater amount of time to process the information.[10] While my sense of time passing was often considerably different from one version to the next, I did not, upon reflection, equate these differences with an overall sense of clock time being altered. In the denser versions, the passing of time felt smoother and more continuous, while in the versions involving fewer players I tended to chunk information into individual clumps of overlapping phrases and move my attention from one to the next. Here my sense of what was to follow was stronger; I anticipated the next chunk of information, creating a sensation of moving constantly toward the next short-lived event, but without the overall sense of continuity that I associated with the denser versions.

Repetition and memory

Multiple performances of the same work within a concert may promote an active kind of listening that encourages the listener to work harder. In the above, extreme example, I was confronted with the same short-duration work multiple times but never permitted to hear the same example twice. Such an experience tests the boundaries of my memory, forcing me to search for differences and similarities between one version and the next. Unlike the more fluid and unpredictable temporal outcomes of *Compatibility hides itself*, proportional representation becomes foregrounded, giving the piece a formal structural coherence. Memory rehearsal is particularly good at teaching us how to listen, and each version is short enough for me to gradually build up a sense of the overall duration each time the piece is reenacted. This duration remains at a consistent eighteen seconds with a short pause of equal duration in between iterations. By listening repeatedly to this event, I am able to predict with some accuracy its length and when it will end. Duration itself therefore becomes prioritized above content, making the notion of *time as a lived experience* central to my understanding of the piece.

Difficulties in perception

While I found it possible to predict the durational spans, building up a comprehensive understanding of the details of each composite part and their relation with each other was considerably more difficult. My initial expectation had been that, through persistent listening through the sixty-three versions, the details contained within each line might be revealed over time. However, after listening over and over to the recording, many of the details of the work remained beyond the reach of my memory. While some of this may be down to my own inabilities as a listener, I propose that there are three aspects of the work which make memorization particularly difficult:

Layering

Since the piece is composed of layers, the different versions offer the possibilities of either perceptual clarity or distortion for the listener depending on the particular combinations of instruments and degrees of density at play. When a particular version consists of only one or two layers, the details of the materials are more clearly perceptible and memorable. In other instances, the surface becomes muddied—some materials becoming buried under others—leading to degrees of textural ambiguity. The register of the particular instrument is particularly significant since the superimposition of lower-pitched instruments leads, rather predictably, to more muddied textures than those in the higher register. These versions are particularly difficult to remember since they appear less distinct from one another.

Changes in or absences of chunking boundaries

Bob Snyder has described how "the formation of phrases creates boundaries, points where things begin and end."[11] He describes this process as chunking.[12] As the notes above demonstrate, it was easier for me to identify boundaries in those versions that contained three or fewer instruments. In most instances of musical perception, such chunking helps us to remember musical events by dividing up information into more easily digestible portions. However, in *511 possible mosaics* the textural surface is multidimensional, active, and prone to constant changes. The kind of listening that this promotes is described by Snyder as follows: "Our sensory organs and thoughts are virtually always in motion. And we are constantly scanning the environment and holding previous scans in short-term memory. Figure-ground relationships are often rapidly changing as part of this motion."[13] As Snyder has said of such music, "Because it is unclear where the chunking boundaries are, it is hard to know how to break the patterns up to retain them as memory."[14] The difficulty in being able to retain these patterns once again prioritizes form over content; I am constantly scanning the surface, alert to each moment and yet unable to recall when and where these events occurred previously.

Interference and memory sabotage

At times, the changes between one version and the next feel slight, resulting in nuanced variations in texture. When a complete alteration in instrumentation occurs, it seems to result in a certain canceling of memory. Over time, as a result of an accumulation of lots of similar types of information, it becomes difficult for me to recollect the details. As I was listening to the piece, I experienced what Snyder has referred to as an "interference effect."[15]

> The disadvantage of a generalised, schema-driven recognition system is that over time, because they are always undergoing the process of being slowly generalised, particular episodic memories of experiences that are similar and fit the same schemas tend to become confused. That is, when we have any type of experience repeatedly, we have great difficulty remembering the details of any particular occurrence, unless they are fairly unusual.[16]

Therefore, what I begin to accrue is not only more concrete information of the original lines in their "pure" or true state but a manifestation of all the possible resultant combinations. Thus, while the focus would appear to be continually closing in—placing the same materials under greater and greater scrutiny—at the same time, the horizon gets wider as the number of different perspectives increases.

Further considerations regarding *Compatibility hides itself* and *511 possible mosaics*

The notated score

The majority of Saunders' short pieces composed during 1996–2000 are single-page scores. The page acts as an operational frame in which events are organized. Although this chapter has been primarily concerned with my perceptual responses to listening to these pieces without the score, I feel that some consideration must be given to the notation itself. The time frame that I perceive phenomenologically cannot be entirely divorced from the spatial aspects of its construction, since the physical limitations of the printed page are intrinsically related to physical aspects of duration. Their materials spread out across several bars that are organized into mosaic-like patterns. Each bar is of the same size and measured with a ruler to create a grid-like structure; a temporal framework into which materials can be placed, examined and redistributed. These elements, I would argue, have a direct bearing on how I hear the materials at play in these works. The strict organization principles at play cannot be immediately discerned (indeed, it is Saunders' intention to obscure these processes to some degree) but its methods of construction are none the less still present. Each event acts as a self-contained unit that plays itself out over time. In the case of *511 possible mosaics*, I am constantly witnessing the relative degrees of compression and attenuation within the grid while in *Compatibility hides itself* I have a sense of the temporal grid itself being stretched or contracted through time.

Aspects of compression

Saunders described his approach to these pieces as "summarising material to represent large scale forms."[17] The composer elaborates further on this in his PhD thesis, explaining that his intention is to maximize content by emulating the structure of a larger work over a much shorter duration. He suggests that this can be achieved by one of two methods: either discarding anything superfluous to the piece in an attempt to focus only on what is absolutely necessary or compressing large amounts of information into a tight space. Since each part is constructed with space in mind, he separates individual gestures by moments of silence, and since presenting a hyper-dense result is the foremost intention, the approach adopted in these works would seem to be the former one.

Any performance of the work must therefore attempt to convey *all of the material* as effectively as possible. Anything that gets lost is to the detriment of the absolute quality of the work. This must include not only the nuances of pitch and the articulation of the meticulously prescribed rhythmic structures but also dynamic distinctions and performance techniques. Such attention to detail may account to a large degree for the poised and highly charged performances discussed here. Working with high degrees of magnification places the emphasis on moment-to-moment interactions, resulting in a heightened sense of awareness and focused level of engagement. I must be poised, like a cat, and ready to spring into action the moment the piece begins.

Accounting for the experience of listening retrospectively

Trying to write about my experience of these pieces while listening to them has proved to be an impossible task; any thoughts I have on the music must be recorded retrospectively. Even in the case of the multiple versions of *511 possible mosaics* performed back-to-back, I was unable to listen and make notes at the same time, such was the level of concentration required while listening. This stands at odds with my previous experience of writing about Feldman's *Piano, Violin, Violin, Cello*, where the act of writing most often took place during the continued listening of the work. In Saunders' works, I have an encounter with time but always feel as if I am playing "catch up" with where I am in the music. Part of the difficulty comes of course from the brevity of these works but can also be attributed to the high degree of information content.

In an unpublished interview with David Osmond Smith, Brian Ferneyhough spoke of the kind of listening that is necessary for his music:

> When anyone says about my music that it's very fast I don't think they mean lots and lots of notes (although they might), but I think more likely they are complaining, or at least asserting, that the music's speed of presentation—of the imagery or the objects in it—is always slightly ahead of our ability to assimilate these objects, so they're extremely resistant. So that requires a greater push, a psychic push on the part of the listener, and so this external act of being slightly behind, and of feeling oneself being slightly behind whilst listening to the new things that are being presented

is a sort of (without trying to be pretentious) meta-listening. I suppose—a sort of listening about listening.[18]

Although Ferneyhough is discussing the moment-by-moment speculative listening that takes place most often over a larger span of time, Saunders' piece, for me, promotes a similar kind of listening experience; the information content is such that I am forced to evaluate the music retrospectively. Saunders said something similar when he commented:

> When the time span of the piece is very close to that of short-term memory, the replaying of the music in the sensory register can be done at a time outside the boundaries of the piece, so that it does not conflict with information gathering. This situation is normally only reserved for the end of compositions. There is a moment when we rewind, perhaps summarising our experience of a piece for a few moments, aware suddenly of the absence of stimulus and the need to catch up.[19]

Interestingly, in Saunders' work this situation is also "reserved for the end of the composition" but it is telling that he does not refer to it as such. Perhaps this is because "the end" occurs at a point when the beginning is still on the horizon, and active within the listener's memory.

Trying not to miss the details of these events demands a great deal of my attention. There is no opportunity to ease into the piece, to acclimatize, to adjust mentally to the sound world created. Unlike in many works, where it is in the opening of the music piece that invites us to listen, here with Saunders' short work I must—if possible—be prepared to listen even before it has begun. The uniqueness of each performance only serves to emphasize this aspect further. To miss out on aspects of the performance is to miss out on an event that will never be recreated in quite the same way. Arguably, this ephemeral quality is equally maintained throughout a performance even when multiple versions of the same piece are performed in concert. If anything, the nuanced differences between one hearing and the next promote slight differences at play and draw attention to slight changes in the proximity of events.

Coming *out of* the piece also requires time, and there is a moment—perhaps only a few seconds—where I feel both *in the piece* and *outside of it*, where I am left with the feeling that the sounds are still acting upon me, physically. It is almost as if there is a short but immeasurable period of time following the final sounding moments of the piece that also belongs to the work, thus extending its clock duration by a few seconds. This occurs even in the versions of *511 possible mosaics* that create a strong sense of closure: the piece still feels *present*, albeit momentarily. For me, this is an indication of the captivating and empowering effect that short-duration works can have.

Closing comments

Revisiting these pieces after a period of some twenty years has been a thought-provoking and strangely nostalgic experience. Ultimately, Saunders' short works remind me that music *needs time* but beg the question, how much time is enough? These are short pieces but they are still long enough to exceed the specious present.[20] There are far shorter works; JLIAT's composition *Still Life #6* (2000), mentioned in Saunders' thesis, lasts a fraction of a second (approximately 0.00002 seconds). Such a work draws upon a conceptual realm of music-making; it is a piece to be imagined or perhaps perceived for just an instant. Saunders' pieces, for me, are about something else: they expand, build, and die. Things happen, even if, as I have discussed earlier, the pieces seem to end almost before they have begun.

Tim Rutherford-Johnson asks: "Can very short work establish a temporal space all of its own, or is it simply another event within the general soundscape?"[21] Taken as singular events, it may be tempting to say that Saunders' pieces could easily become subsumed into the "general landscape." As Michael Rofe has said, "It takes time to hear music, and it takes interactions between the temporal domains of past, present and future to detect patterns in, and ascribe significance to, music."[22] Do these early short works by Saunders allow enough time for the interactions that Rofe speaks of to become meaningful? For me, these works really become meaningful when heard in sets or where repeated hearings are possible. When taken as a collection of multiple iterations, it is possible to see Saunders' pieces in a different light: in a space of their own. Saunders himself was keen to promote multiple listenings during a concert, and in hearing the same piece more than once, the listener is invited to participate in an active kind of listening. This is not unlike the experience of listening to late Feldman described in the last chapter, in which I enter into a perceptual game of recollection. When the last notes of Feldman's *Piano, Violin, Viola, Cello* die away, a space opens up for reflection. In these short pieces by Saunders, I also find myself with space to reflect on a musical experience that challenges the conventions of form and structure. The moment of silence that follows the piece is no less profound than the piece itself. Time relaxes, opens up, and leads me to a point of reflection.

Notes

1   James Saunders, "Developing a Modular Approach to Music" (PhD diss., University of Huddersfield), 3.
2   Ibid., 25.

3   Richard Kostelanetz, *Conversing with Cage* (New York: Routledge, 2003), 232.
4   James Saunders, e-mail message to author, November 18, 2017.
5   Saunders, "Developing a Modular Approach," 41.
6   Ibid., 42.
7   Ibid., 48.
8   There is also a 512th version, with no players, performed by 175 East. This version was added because the father of one of the ensemble members, a mathematician, pointed out the anomaly.
9   Saunders, "Developing a Modular Approach," 48.
10 Barbara R. Barry, *Musical Time: The Sense of Order* (Stuyvesant, New York: Pendragon Press, 1990), 132.
11 Bob Snyder, *Music and Memory: An Introduction* (Cambridge, MA: The MIT Press, 2000), 59.
12 Ibid., 257.
13 Ibid., 51.
14 Ibid., 66.
15 Ibid., 260.
16 Ibid., 99.
17 Saunders, "Developing a Modular Approach," 41.
18 Brian Ferneyhough, interview by David Osmond-Smith, BBC Concert Hall, Broadcasting House, London, June 29, 1993, transcript by James Gardner.
19 Saunders, "Developing a Modular Approach," 14.
20 See Jonathan Kramer, *The Time of Music* (New York: Schirmer Books, 1988), 371–374.
21 Tim Rutherford-Johnson, *Music after the Fall: Modern Composition and Culture since 1989* (Oakland, CA: University of California Press, 2017), 86.
22 Michael Rofe, "Dualisms of Time," *Contemporary Music Review* 33, no. 4 (2014): 341, http://dx.doi.org.libaccess.hud.ac.uk/10.1080/07494467.2014.977024.

Postlude to Chapter Two

Jennie Gottschalk

In a conversation about this piece, Bryn and I discussed the relevance of Wallace Stevens' poem, "13 Ways of Looking at a Blackbird." Saunders' piece also names a number of possibilities—the 511 possible combinations of nine instruments, from solo to all nine. My listening experience of the piece is similarly best presented as a number of ways of receiving and considering this material, even with reference to a single recording and ordering of combinations by a single ensemble. They would multiply even further various other possible presentations of the work.

My own ways of thinking about this piece changed quite a bit as I listened to successive iterations. While I first heard instrumental characters, I then realized that the instruments' roles shifted depending on which of them were playing together. The material transforms in its context, depending on which other instruments are playing around it. My attempts to make sense of the effects of the various juxtapositions of instrumental parts, and in particular my pausing in between each segment, gave each of them a sense of presence which outweighed anything I could have anticipated based on its short duration.

I also didn't yet understand that each mosaic was the same length, drawn from the exact same material. But the melodic and gestural nature stood as a contradiction to the brevity of each segment. I wrote, "The types of interplays between instruments (not necessarily interactions) don't affect my sense of duration in particular, but my sense of the density or shape or trajectory of that duration."

That got me on the track of listening for shapes. And why not? That's what I heard, or envisioned, in the listening for my Tsunoda chapter, and also in the form of the Möller piece. #070 was a "highly gestural, diagonal sort of shape," I wrote, and "leaves off with a sense of that same motion continuing (still traveling in lines from low/percussive to high)." #020 was "hovering without a foundation, inconclusive," and the clarinet, bass clarinet, and trombone in #075 were "tangled up together." In #039, there was a "wide gulf" between the bass trombone and the double bass. This gulf was not registral but textural.

The interplay between the instruments often came across as pushes and pulls, or pressures. The instruments in #141 were "competing impulses," where #100 struck a more balanced, even relationship between the instruments. These reactions may be entirely subjective, and even somewhat without justification. But I present them here as multiple ways of hearing, parallel to Stevens' thirteen ways of looking.

Still another basis of comparison was to the verbal or dramatic. #054 was prosaic, #018 was a series of questions, and in the bass trombone's solo, material that seemed comedic in an ensemble took on pathos in solitude.

All of these observations were made based on the first half of the 22-minute recording of 175 East's performance. I would play a twenty-second track, pause, write something down, then play another one. Gradually my attention began to flag, until I was leaving multiple instances blank. As Richard and I began to discuss the piece, several key points about the work's construction came into view, resulting in a much richer listening experience that followed. Bryn's stamina was much greater than mine, as he wrote rather extensively about each instance. Interestingly, his comments are far more technical than they were for the Feldman piece, as if he's taking a microscope to these tiny specimens. Like me, he took each combination on its own terms, finding that "each new version would 'cleanse the palate'" and allow him to "hear the piece afresh."

Richard pointed out that with "something like four, five instruments plus … they don't sound as different to each other. But when you have a solo or two instruments playing off of each other, it suddenly kind of refocuses you." In our conversation, I also realized that there was a type of inversion: When fewer instruments were playing, more information was revealed. A solo presents one definite piece of the whole, where an actual presentation of all nine instruments (which was not present in this recording) would be so saturated with information that it could not be disentangled. Bryn speaks of instrumental parts being alternately "subsumed" or "buried" and "excavated." Richard said, "The material was always actually kind of being hindered, contained, and then that for me just really pushed it through each time, with the larger ensembles." There were far fewer rests or pauses with the more composite versions, and for me also, the more populated versions felt significantly shorter, since they took on more of a sense of shape and momentum. As Richard put it, the masking of instruments by one another "condenses the temporal space." Bryn heard the version with all six instruments as "a chunking of materials."

The pieces also sounded more similar to me when they were heard in larger sets, rather than separated. In this recording, there are sixty-three of them in a row, with rather short silences between each one. That type of configuration was likely aligned with Saunders' intention, and I went against it in my early listening with long pauses for writing between each track. I got lost in the details until a sort of fatigue took over and I listened to more without stopping. Then a clump of them with mostly four or more instruments became very difficult for me to tell apart. Bryn noted a similar experience around 9:47: "It is becoming increasingly difficult to focus in on the individual identity of each version as concentration becomes an issue." His attention, like mine, was restored with the clarinet solo.

When I went back to listen after discussing the piece, it was an almost entirely different experience. I went into this listening with a clear sense that each instrument played a single, unchanging layer of an incomprehensible whole. Each part contained several pieces of the puzzle (or tiles of the mosaic, to use Saunders' analogy). I also knew that the duration of each segment was essentially identical, which helped to secure my listening experience. It gave an aspect of certainty. One thing at least—total duration of each segment— was consistent. Going into this second listening, I began to hear parts of an elusive whole, rather than trying to track the intricate interactions between the various instruments. While coming to terms with the fact that the whole was never going to be apparent to me, I began to feel that I could achieve an abstracted sense of it through these multiple presentations. I began to listen globally, from one track to the next, rather than attempting to document the peculiarities of each iteration. Halfway through this listening, I wrote, "I'm listening back to an overlay of textures, trying to make sense of it as a whole." That experience was far richer and far less tiring. I wrote that each mosaic "is intricate, a tiny series of jewels, massive potential despite being the same elements." I compared the two listening experiences to "swimming in a big pool of possibilities versus trying to recall multiple tidepools of activity." Bryn wrote about the inability to reflect on any of the pieces during its presentation, but only reflecting in retrospect. My best view of the more global unfolding of events was similarly retrospective.

Macro and micro modes of listening are in such an interesting tension between these two experiences of the piece. Listening one way is just about opposite from listening to the other. I approached my second listening as perspectives on a massive whole. Time passed very quickly, slipping through my fingers as I tried to glean information from the successive views, as if I were running around a sculpture, trying to hold the entire image in mind. Near the end of the recording, I began to imagine some of the absent instruments along with the present ones. But the totality of the layers and potential interactions remained out of sight. The presentation of the work seemed to have begun before I arrived, leaving me struggling to catch up, and to have ended without revealing itself.

My sense of the dimensions of the work began with a hypothetical, what Richard called an "abstract idea of a short piece, something under 20 seconds." A set of such pieces—or so I thought before listening—would be a collection of tiny jewels, easily comprehended in a single view and then compared one to another. In the actual event, these iterations of the work made me successively less sure of the nature of the work as a whole. In my dawning apprehension of the work's behavior, it became a much more significant temporal and musical experience than I had anticipated.

CHAPTER THREE

Separation and Continuity in Chiyoko Szlavnics' *Gradients of Detail*

Richard Glover

This chapter will explore how Canadian composer Chiyoko Szlavnics' piece for string quartet, *Gradients of Detail* (2005/6), can yield a wide variety of temporal experiences, and how its relatively reduced material results in an amplified, close listening which further reinforces a broad range of temporalities. I will be using the Asasello Quartet's recording, released on World Edition,[1] as the textual reference for this chapter.

Szlavnics employed a very particular mode of compositional strategy for this piece, as she has with others from this period, but this method of construction is not one which will inform the following discussion. This will be returned to at the end of this chapter in order to explore alignments or conflicts, but Szlavnics' methodology should not be seen as underpinning the approach to the discussion of temporal experiences undergone while listening to the piece.

In order for the considerations of listening perception to take a primary role, along with the nature of the performance by the Asasello Quartet, this analysis will not be related to the score of the piece, but rather the experience of the music, *as heard*. Considerations of composer intention are therefore balanced alongside aspects of the sound, and action, of performance.

As much of the piece employs the same kinds of sonic elements and textures throughout, this provided a fruitful platform to reflect upon the temporal experience, through the lens of composer James Tenney's application of temporal gestalts (TGs). Tenney himself explored sustained textures in many of his pieces, and so we see in Szlavnics (herself a student of Tenney's) an interest in exploring sustained tone environments, although with an entirely individual, idiosyncratic approach to their conception, construction, and implementation in performance. This is music with nuanced changes, in which micro-level shifts are amplified and have wider ramifications than in more overtly varied, gestural-dramatic musics.

Listening commentary

This chapter will begin with a personal account of a single listening through to *Gradients of Detail*, which explores my own perceptions as a listener to the recorded performance of this music. The language used is an attempt to describe responses purely to the auditory experience rather than references to external elements such as the score, compositional methodology, and other aspects of the music actualization process.

Following handwritten documentation of these experiences during the listening, the text has been edited to clarify the points made within the documentation.

* * *

As harmonic intervals gradually appear from slow glissandi, these shifts provide a forward momentum to the temporal flow
Bow changes add a sense of movement, liveliness
They increase in density—the flow slows down—and beating patterns seem to expand, widen the present
A reference point is provided by a clear harmonic interval; this gives me a sense of stability after the continual pitch change
Gradual density change
Short glissandi provide movement, acceleration
I become more conscious of the drone underneath—it seems to counter the movement from the glissandi, there is a feeling of deceleration, reining the flow in
A new drone pitch constrains the flow even further
Followed by a glissando, into a stable harmonic interval—the teleology of that long gesture pushes the flow forward
Similar harmonies continue
A higher density is slowly reached, acoustic beats expand the present moment, it contracts suddenly but then expands again following another sequence of beats, but this time it feels different to before

A stable interval follows, now it seems to sit, solidify for a long time

Lighter density prompts closer, more focused listening, there is more detail in the sound to be explored—as I seem to wade into the details of the sound, I somehow am able to take a long, protracted time to do this; I am made aware of the present expanding to invite me in further

Higher density of materials then seems to bring attention to movement, dynamism again

A very close glissando which moves on through a unison, the pace of my experience heightens, intensifies

A long pause—I am made aware that there has only been continuous sound up until this moment—it extends on and on, extraordinarily long

Followed by a high-dense cluster which suggests a more fluid, quicker experience

Shorter pauses, different lengths, although these prove very difficult to compare

A lower pitch cluster extends this moment

I quickly lose track of how many pauses there are

A higher density creates added forward motion; a stronger perception of bowing on the instruments reinforces this momentum

A closer pitch cluster, even a faint sensation of beating patterns expands the moment

There are much longer pauses now—it is difficult to recollect ordering of what has just been heard, and I very quickly become disorientated

Mid-register cluster again, but heightened movement, tension, as it follows the previous section of long silences

Low cello drone counteracts the mid-register—again, lighter density, a solo drone, equates to a finer grain, prompting much closer perceptual inspection

Short pauses, then louder material; I experience this as much stronger intensity, a stronger bow pressure, even though it may not be significantly louder

Single full sound, no detail, smooth and consistent

This is then joined by others, heavier density, which now slows down—and granulates—my experience

Long, extended silence—sense of it being much longer than previous silences

Followed by a mid-register cluster, rather than high pitch, and the pacing now feels much slower

Sudden isolated pizzicato suggests closing of one section, beginning of another

Significantly longer glissandi, experienced as a much longer section

Constant, confusing interplay between expansive beating patterns, and heightened, intensified tension as a harmonic interval endpoint may be approaching

Interplay continues on and on; the shorter section before the pizzicato results in this experience seeming much more fraught, with multiple shifting temporalities, an extraordinary conflict between my different faculties of temporal sensation

Endpoint of glissandi is a just-tuned major third which provides stability; this now suggests a much quicker progressive flow
This is followed by higher density; more frequent, noticeable bow changes prompt a closer listening attention to the additional detail, but there is an overall sense of greater movement
A sustained section of beating patterns, there are both constant pulses and patterns of transforming rhythms, generating a temporal flow which is rocking, lilting, as it ebbs and flows
A delicate, thin unison prompts close listening attention to detail in performance
Pizzicato again suggests a partial section closure, and a renewal of movement—it seems to induce a faster temporal flow in whatever will follow
I become aware of a low drone; I hear it as faster-paced—as if this drone is quickly dissipating the energy from the pizzicato
Following silence feels very long, possibly longer than before—it is very difficult to compare
Very high-pitch cluster does not suggest quick movement as before; it now seems much more rooted, and I am made aware of the lack of forward momentum which similar material prompted previously

I am aware that my ability to judge relative duration is now significantly impaired, particularly because of long silences followed by sustained pitch clusters

A mid-high, full string sound suggests a quickening of pace—there is a pointed clarity in the sound now, rather than the "patchwork" high cluster just heard
A unison then extends for seemingly much longer than any of the previous silences—I seem to be transforming the previous-experienced steadiness, invariability, of the drone into a sense of movement, perhaps as a result of the movement experienced in other recent material. There is no sense of "timelessness"; instead, it is pulling me forward through the temporal flow
A very slow glissando amplifies this sense; I continue to experience an intensifying forward motion
A higher density of lines in the glissandi gesture means it is harder to hear a reference point, any sort of detail, which slowly shifts my experience to more of an expanded present; any sense of my being propelled forward by the music dissipates
A mid-low drone now amplifies this new sense of a "fixed expansion" further

A lower glissando then provides counterpoint, and a graininess in the string sound contrasts with smooth sustained sound; the fixed expansion dissolves away to a gentle temporal flow

Higher densities of glissandi then prompt me to lose a reference point again; it is difficult to perceive section-duration, but duration feels very different to the earlier section of constant, confusing interplay. The lower register has more detail: there are many more bow changes and contrasts in bow pressure

A quieter sound seems to significantly slow the temporal flow; emanating from the dense complex network just heard, this seems like a sound external to the piece itself

Final cello drone, while suddenly contrasting with cluster above, actually seems to continue at a similar pace of experience as with harmonic interval just before, as awareness of bow movement becomes the primary driver for attention here. Bow movements become sweeps, and any temporal flow is structured by the performers' bowing arm action

✷ ✷ ✷

For a piece with such limited use of material throughout (that is to say, the content is essentially sustained tones separated by silences), the listening commentary demonstrates that there is an exceptional amount of variety and transformation in the temporal response I experienced when listening to it. In the commentary, I have taken the *flow* of the temporal experience as a base point, which was a linguistic tool emerging early on from the material; it is entirely possible for another temporal model to be utilized as appropriate with a contrasting piece. Couzens Hoy writes how, "[i]f temporality is a flow, then duration is a feature of the flow,"[2] and as such I tend toward reflection on certain sectional durations, in order to consider my capacity for durational awareness in the face of an ever-changing temporal flow.

There are many aspects to remark upon from the listening commentary. Some of the priorities as regard discussion on temporal experience are:

- The sudden shifts in listening focus are prompted by a heightened *detail* in the sound; the same kind of texture was heard at various points in the piece, but the heightened sense of the performer, or even *humanity*, in the sound, resulted in a contrasting listening experience.

- The appearance of sustained, stable harmonic intervals provides multiple contrasting temporal experiences.

- Sustained pitches, and in particular those in the low registers, are experienced very differently throughout. The listening experience appears to be heavily dependent upon any preceding material— for instance, how can two sustained tones, played by the same instrument, seem faster, or slower, compared to one another?

- The varying duration of silences impacts any material which follows that silence, and entangles temporal experiences.

- Pizzicato disrupts the temporal flow and impacts heavily upon my experience over the subsequent brief window of time.

- I compare a present experience with previous experiences more as the piece continues (as might perhaps be expected—there is more to compare); however, I do not know what I should be comparing, as there is no clear "primary material" or sequence of events which dominates the experience.

While there is clearly no position to draw fixed conclusions from these points, further discussion can focus upon why these contrasting temporal experiences might be prompted by particular materials, or, conversely, why particular materials might prompt contrasting materials at different moments within a piece.

I use the phrase "reference point" many times, yet what might a reference point constitute in a piece with such minimal materials as this? Elements such as the onset of an extended silence, or of sound following a silence, are clearly points to recall, to reference back. But changing densities of pitch clusters, emerging detail of sound through aspects of the performance, and acoustic phenomena seem to occasionally provide points to demarcate sections, or with which to connect; there is never an absolute consistency over what these elements should be, as it is entirely context-dependent, and it seems a feature of the documentation that the desire, or need, to grasp at a reference point is intensified at certain sections and lessened at others.

* * *

In my individual reflective text, I have treated all aspects of the auditory material equally, rather than discussing aspects of the sound which were composed (e.g., section duration and glissando range) and those which arise from performative actions (specific bow changes, changes in bow pressure, and beating patterns). The discussion will now focus upon these two different aspect groupings as distinct from one another, in order to understand further the impact of the act of performance upon the temporal experience. These will be grouped as follows:

Composed elements:

- Sonority/density of held tones and glissandi

- Register

- Pizzicati

Elements arising from performance:

- Bowing
- Beating patterns

These will each be discussed in turn utilizing the notion of TGs to prompt an understanding—or at least, a heightened focus—upon different temporal experiences offered by these aspects. Through these discussions, I will also encompass, either specifically or more broadly, the overriding concerns from the reflective text: how held tones and intervals are experienced differently throughout the piece, how actions in performance can impact upon an experience, the roles of the pizzicato and silences in disrupting and informing the future temporal flow, and how all these aspects prompt further comparison, recall, and reference as the piece continues.

Similarly, contrasting with the reflective text, the discussion will not be concerned with a chronological account of elements within the piece, but rather will shift back and forth between commonalities, exploring similarities and difference of types of material across the piece.

Sonority/density of held tones and glissandi

Within *Gradients of Detail*, "held tones and glissandi" encapsulate the range of textures from a sustained tone sounded by a single instrument, unison sustained tones played by two or more instruments, close clusters of pitches played by two or more instruments without a determinate pitch interval, and clusters of wider intervals more easily recognized as specific harmonies, played by two or more instruments. Thus changing densities on unisons, become changing sonorities when expanded out to clusters, which become harmonies when expanded further to make perceptible intervals.

There are also two types of sustained tone: one with a consistent pitch (held tone, or drone), and one with variable pitch (glissando). While these can both engender very different temporalities in a listener, often we hear them simultaneously in *Gradients of Detail*, to the point that it is not worth continuing to describe them separately, except for a few very specific points and sections.

The first section of the piece is undifferentiated; there are drones, and glissandi of different rates, occurring in different textures throughout. The wider discernable intervals (usually major thirds) are reference points, which I often experienced as prompting a sense of rest, or slowing down, but aside from these the section is largely one fluid sustained texture which ends with a silence.

My observations here relating to the blurring of elements, and the manner in which they prompt different temporal responses from me and impact upon surrounding elements, have led me to consider the implications of James Tenney's use of temporal gestalts in the experience of music, and how that might reveal further aspects about *Gradients of Detail*.

Tenney drew upon the work of the German Gestalt psychologists of the 1930s in his master's thesis in 1964, later published as *Meta-Hodos*, which was appended by an additional section for the larger text *META Meta-Hodos* in 1988.[3] These theories were then developed upon further using computer modeling in the article *Temporal Gestalt Perception in Music*, written with Larry Polansky, appearing in the *Journal of Music Theory* in 1980.[4]

Tenney's use of a TG is that of a unit of composition, which has defined starting and end points. TGs can be measured using various parameters, and most often applied from score analysis, as Tenney does frequently within *Meta-Hodos*. He demonstrates how the music can be chunked up depending on various factors, and it is primarily driven by the manner in which our perceptual processes, as listeners, interpret the composed material. For this discussion, I am beginning with the auditory experience of *Gradients of Detail* and drawing out interpretations of TGs from my own perceptual observations. Tenney does include what he terms the "subjective set" alongside other conditions brought to the listening situation, which includes any listeners' experiences, cultures, habits, and so on, which may inform their own, unique response to a piece of music. As Brian Belet states, "For Tenney, the listener's subjective perception is required to create the distinctions between formal TG levels and to distinguish between events on a given level."[5] While the composer creates the potential for music, and the performer brings the music into aural reality, it is the listener who actually interprets the sounds and then creates the resultant structure and relationships.

Tenney used the two terms *proximity* and *similarity* as tools in his theory, to elucidate the manner in which TGs may be distinguished from one another. Proximity describes situations where elements group themselves by their distribution across time, such that sounds separated by time-space would be experienced as separate TGs. Similarity means that elements with relative likeness in sonic parameters such as pitch, timbre, and dynamic will be grouped together.

Tenney's TGs have three perceived time references: the time before the TG, the TG itself, and then the time after the TG,[6] in a similar fashion to Merleau-Ponty's model of retention and protention as being as much a part of experience as Husserl's "primal impression";[7] what interests me here, in this application of TGs, is the manner in which I as a listener comprehend a new primal impression as affecting my awareness of the temporal experience. What *affects* my awareness of my own experience, and how?

One route of exploring TGs here is to identify parts within the larger, fluid sustained texture described above which contain one or more glissandi and those which are comprised entirely of sustained tones. The experience of a held tone after a glissando up or down to it (which may be experienced as some form of destination tone) can result in experiencing the flow of the glissando through the held tone, most potently in the initial stages of that held tone. When the held tones range over a more easily discernable (i.e. wider) interval, this sense of the motion of the glissando resonating through into the held note is less prominent, but when glissandi lead into a pitch cluster, or for example a semitone, then the sense of movement within that cluster is much more palpable (additionally from the beating patterns, to be discussed later). The discrete ending of one TG and movement into another was far less clear for me: the similarity is continued through, and thus it becomes difficult to confidently state that a glissando is a separate TG to the held tones into which it leads. This similarity between the glissando and the held tone interval (when smaller) then served to expand the temporal horizon outward, and a present was experienced as occurring over a longer duration. When a wider interval was achieved, there was a greater perceptual difference to the blurring from the glissando, and thus I experienced the two as discrete TGs, with their own separate temporal flows and distinct methods of comprehending duration.

I found that movements from held tones and glissandi tended to be much more distinct, although again when intervals are closer in pitch, or very close clusters, then the impact of the move to a glissando seemed to be lessened. However, I found that held tones over a certain duration were always eventually experienced as rescinding the flow of time, or beginning to move outward rather than an omnidirectional arrow of time, and when this is followed by a glissando—in whatever degree of suddenness—the experience was distinctive; a temporal flow was reestablished by the pitch movement in the glissando, and the continually moving interval informed the manner in which temporality shifted.

A factor to be superimposed onto these considerations is the density of these elements. When the density of tones remains the same from glissando to held tones, there is far less distinction than when an instrument drops out once, for example, and a unison or interval is achieved; in the latter scenario, there is a lessening of a sense of movement and temporality shifts to a less strident forward motion. When two glissandi are joined by a third, this amplified the intensity for me, inducing a visceral sonic change within the detail of the sound, and again prompted greater temporal excitation.

In an extended interplay of these changing elements (held intervals, glissandi, solo instrument, four instruments, and multiple instrument unisons) without break, this prompts a platform of ever-changing temporalities, within a narrow band of possibilities; the similarities between the different elements control the extent to which they may be determined as separate TGs, but as the sound is always comprising sustained tones (of fixed pitch or glissandi), this renders the whole section as being perceived as one higher-level TG. Tenney used the word "holarchical" to describe this broader TG which encompassed smaller elements, and this first section of *Gradients of Detail* is a patchwork of lower-level TGs with varying levels of similarity, but which each produce their own transformative impacts upon the temporal experience.

Different speeds of glissandi certainly have the ability to push the temporal flow at a faster rate, but my recall of similar long glissandi seems to prompt these as slower still. Therefore, slow movements from unison outward are such a common feature of the piece that each new time this occurs (from either the whole quartet or two or three instruments) they seem to occur over a longer duration.

Interestingly, Szlavnics has said that drone-like music is not something she is interested in, but tends toward dynamic inner structures with composed moving parts, due to her desire to create "clear, strong forms";[8] this predilection toward slow glissandi rather than creating music solely of drones provided for me very distinct, transformative temporal experiences, and a clarity in recalling recent gestures, yet richly difficult to comprehend across broader time spans.

Register

The majority of the piece occurs within what is heard as the center of the pitch register; it is only later in the piece that the listener's attention can be drawn to this facet, however, as low sustaining cello and high violin clusters are heard. Indeed, the piece ends with a low cello pitch, thus again bringing an awareness of attention upon this difference, and for me prompting a gradual decrease in temporal flow in response to the higher, more strained sounds in the strings heard throughout many earlier parts of the piece.

It is interesting to consider the role of these shifts of register upon the listener's temporal experience; composers are made aware through their practice of the heightened tension of sudden, dramatic registral changes, but how might these impact upon a temporal flow, or a listener's ability to both contextualize new material and recall details from previous recent or more distant material? While the overall nature of movement of gestures in *Gradients of Detail* is very gradual, the impact of the registral shifts is significant; indeed, the high-pitch cluster heard after one of the longer silences brings about a major change in the nature of the music, even though its dynamic, performance technique and duration, remains the same as that pitched material which preceded the silence before it.

Overall, I heard a shift to a higher-pitch cluster as a heightening of intensity, and this consequently prompted a forward propulsion in the temporal flow, whereas a shift to a lower-pitch cluster acted as a restraining action upon the temporal flow, seeming to increase a sense of inertia. What is noticeable in *Gradients of Detail* is how often the higher pitches are heard in clusters, and as such higher densities, while lower pitches are heard as single sustained tones on fixed pitches. Therefore, when there are sudden shifts to higher registers, I focused upon the interplay within that cluster, and the higher density had a more visceral impact upon the sonic surface; when sudden lower register changes were experienced, the solo instrumental sound remained more in the background of my focus and thus didn't prompt such an immediacy and forward propulsion in the temporal flow.

Pizzicati

Finally, it is important to mention the two pizzicato events which occur within the piece. These are entirely unexpected, have the effect of disrupting the temporal flow, and provide two of the clearest, differentiated reference markers experienced throughout the piece. It becomes very difficult to recall which other events occurred before and after these pizzicati, as they seem to perform a kind of erasure upon my memory; not everything is wiped, but rather the suddenness of the pizzicati seems to render previous material as more difficult to distinguish. The second pizzicato necessarily brings reminiscences of the first, but even here I found it hard to recollect how long ago that first pizzicato appeared, and in what context, as the second pulled me very quickly into the immediate present.

There is an aspect of TGs referenced earlier by Belet which is relevant to the pizzicati, stating that TGs have three perceived time references: the time before the TG, the TG itself, and then the time after the TG. There is certainly a similarity here in how I documented the moments of pizzicati in the listening commentary; the experienced temporalities of each pizzicato in *Gradients of Detail* don't seem to simply cover the duration of the pizzicati—obviously, very short in comparison to all the other sustained tones and silences—but instead, the pizzicati seem to shape the temporality of particularly the succeeding material, often by anchoring in an added momentum to the drone, pitch cluster, or whatever follows.

Perceptions of performativity

Having discussed the elements of the piece which are composed, I now want to explore those aspects of the *performance* of *Gradients of Detail*, which are not gleaned from the score, and are entirely unique to the Asasello recording.

How do these indeterminate performance idiosyncrasies overlay onto the instructions of the piece (given to the performers), as best we can infer them from the sound? Do these aspects reinforce the temporal experience we would gain from the intentionality we can infer from the construction (a long glissando *without* retakes of the bow), or render a different, or enhanced, or divergent, experience? And yet, beating patterns and bow changes clearly *are* intended by the composer, but are simply not written in. What tension is there, in terms of temporality, between these and the composed aspects?

This is considerably different to composers of music of gradual change who create their music using electronics—digital or analogue—such as Éliane Radigue, Catherine Lamb, or Laurie Spiegel. The music of these composers is designed to create a very smooth surface, with beating patterns held consistently over a certain duration—the composer's intentionality is clear. With *Gradients of Detail* and other similar pieces for unstable human-controlled interfaces such as those in a string quartet, these acoustic phenomena and instrumental techniques are a result of both rehearsal decisions made by the performers and the specific performance actions carried out at the time the recording was made, unique to that performance occasion.

Bowing

My exploration of the temporal experience of this piece utilizing the audio recording rather than the score resulted in a much closer connection to the performative actions made by the players. One of the most apparent of these is the bowing actions of each of the four string players. Particularly evident in the sustained textures of *Gradients of Detail* are the details in the bow changes, in which the beginning of each new bow prompts a perceivable attack—however slight—with a change in bow pressure, which can also include a reduction in bow pressure toward the end of the previous bow. While this is a feature of many other sustained tone pieces for strings, for instance pieces by Alvin Lucier such as *Navigations for Strings* (1992) and *Slices* (2007), the higher clusters in *Gradients of Detail* render this phenomena particularly apparent, in which very thin notes high up in the violin register are more vulnerable to changes of bow pressure toward the end of the bow, and attacks at the beginning of a new bow are more difficult to conceal. Consistency of bow pressure throughout a bow is more generally exposed in these pitches, and can result in a considerably changeable, complex actioning of simple compositional ideas.

While there are a number of points in *Gradients of Detail* where the Asasello Quartet have clearly consciously decided on a unison down bow—again, however slight—there are necessarily plenty of moments where individual players must retake their bow, against the sustained sound of other players' notes, as individual notes begin and end at different points in time. I found myself questioning whether these bow changes do impact upon temporal experience, and if they might blend together to form some kind of meta-temporal relationship (what Tenney would describe as a higher-level TG). Each bow change is a rearticulation of a tone; it necessarily brings along a movement—indeed, the movement of the action is effectively conveyed in the sound of the attack—and thus I myself become much more aware of the movement, and dynamism, of the string sound.

The continual reconfigurations of the textures caused by bow takes mean that there is less of an immobility about the sustained tones within the piece which would result in an expanding present. This expanded present seems to provide a greater aural surface area which can be perceived in detail, and a more active temporal flow results in less close perceptual focus and a wider comprehension of the syntax generated by these bow changes. These bow changes occasionally coincide to form a network of attacks, which depending on their relative proximity in time can suggest a quickening of temporal flow, or sometimes the opposite if there is an overall move from fast to slow of the frequency of bow changes over time.

Beating patterns

Acoustic beating patterns, which arise between two or more sustained pitches in close proximity with one another, appear at various points within *Gradients of Detail* due to the slow glissandi which converge upon fixed pitches, and sometimes continue moving past them. Where they appear, which is usually once a texture has been instigated, and the listener has become familiar with the global sonority, I experienced them in a similar way to the glissandi, which aligned with the notion of a TG. Here, however, the duration of the beating gestalt seemed to be superimposed upon the existing temporality of the harmonic sonorities in the music, as if there were then multiple temporalities at play. Thus, the nature of those beats can impact upon the listener's sense of temporal flow within a piece, particularly when consideration is given toward these beats as being something external, or separate, to the smooth continuity of the sustained tones and glissandi. The beats are a "product" of these materials; they are not played by another performer, but are a result of *combinations* of materials, which is why they provide a fertile subject to consider here.

While any composer who deploys this kind of material does so knowing that beating patterns will occur, the specific nature of those beats are unknown, as a result of the performers' actions and the acoustic environment. Particular indeterminate aspects include the following:

- What different speeds are generated? (beating patterns slow down as pitches converge)

- If three or four instruments are playing close together, which patterns will dominate, and which will blend together?

- As beating patterns also rely on the consistency of players' bowing action, what are the ranges of difference between beating speeds as a result of any inconsistency in bow action?

Some of Alvin Lucier's music from the 1990s such as *Wind Shadows* (1995)[9] attempted to address these issues by simply stating the number of beating patterns to be heard above each bar; however, here the number of instruments is pared down, and crucially glissandi are present only to help shift to a new beating pattern, rather than being a focus in and of themselves as with *Gradients of Detail*. Lucier's intention is to reveal the different speeds of beating patterns in the performance, whereas Szlavnics is intending something quite different, as borne out by the inclusion of various glissandi-focused gestures, silences, and harmonies throughout. She does not, and cannot, include numerals in a score to indicate specific beating patterns due to the disruption of that aim by these other factors; beating patterns are clearly included as a *result* of transforming pitch clusters, rather than as an end in themselves.

An electronic studio composer has the ability to bypass these aspects and sculpt very specific beating patterns, and polyrhythmic textures of different layers of beating patterns, while being able to be fairly certain about the resultant audible beating pattern numbers (although the potential of the realization space to impact upon those patterns remains present). Interestingly, Szlavnics went on to create two electronic pieces in 2010 (*Interior Landscapes II A* and *B*) which layer up twenty-one pairs of sine waves to generate dense textures of multiple beating patterns.

Szlavnics herself admits that even the consideration of controlling rates of beating did not occur to her until she started working on the *Interior Landscapes* pieces, and although she has wanted to experiment more with electronic pieces following these, she recognizes that for her, the precision poses the danger of beating rates being too mechanically precise.[10] Her own evolution in thinking here demonstrates a new willingness to create teleological pathways out of specific sculpted beating patterns within dense textures. She asks the question, "how does one create a system to produce rates of beating that are musically meaningful?"[11] and considers whether similar pieces could be created with a pedagogical aspect to educate listeners further about the relationship between sound waves and periodicity. However, she has since stated that I find "'the mechanical' to be too regulating of our own corporeal systems ... [a]nd since sine waves are particularly penetrating, I find it disturbing when they 'stand still', that is, when there is an absence of change ... [p]erhaps because everything always does change,"[12] so she is as much, if not more, interested in how human performers generate their own shifting beating patterns through their own organicism, rather than these patterns being predefined beforehand. Ryoji Ikeda's music discussed in the next chapter exemplifies the contrary position to this, in which rhythmically consistent electronically generated pulses quickly recede to the perceptual background as their absolute uniformity conveys Szlavnics' "mechanical" nature.

The question remains: How do these *performed* beating patterns impact upon my temporal experience? In what way does the instability of these beats, their inconsistency (as, say, a glissando approaches a unison, the beats do not smoothly move from slow to fast, as bow changes and necessary instability in tuning, impacts upon the beat audibility), prompt changes in the temporal flow? When my perception changes from focusing on bow hair upon string to audible beating patterns, this is a noticeable shift in itself; there is a sense of a push, which takes the listener out of the realm of gradually moving lines, and into a rhythmic continuum (Lucier has often talked about his fascination with the idea that pitch can create rhythm).[13] This creates a new reference point, but not one which is easily marked; there is no sense of this as a new section, and thus time-ordering is not bolstered but rather somewhat obfuscated. We may be clear in our knowledge that beats are happening, or have happened, but it is difficult to recall their nature. This seems to be due to their nature as phenomena generated by the combination of other, intentional elements: I don't sense that a performer is playing them; therefore, they are an external occurrence. Consider how different this is to knowing a composer of an electronic piece intends for you to hear specifically 3.5 beats per second, at a precise moment within the piece. This clear indeterminacy results in beats acting as occurrences within the temporal flow, rather than maintaining the disruptive significance of silences, or shifts to perceivable intervals.

There are numerous increases in beating patterns which heighten and intensify the temporal flow, particularly when this increase happens very quickly due to faster glissandi. Similarly, a performer's tendency to roll their finger onto the destination pitch can result in fast beating patterns, as well as simply if the interval between pitches are further apart, thus generating faster beating patterns; however, the sense that performers' actions are bringing about these moments of intensification renders the increase of the flow more acute for me. This is all despite the fact that the composed glissandi are moving at a much slower pace than the beating patterns which are occurring in the sounding material.

Silence

There are nine silences throughout *Gradients of Detail*, and each of these prompted different experiences of temporality within me, mostly due to the material preceding the silence which affected the listening perspective I employed as the silence began. The longest one, almost halfway through the piece, allows a significant amount of time for introspection of what I have just heard, and how I am experiencing the present silence. I describe it as seeming "extraordinarily long" in the listening commentary, as I started to wonder more whether or not the instruments would even return, and what material they would play. Upon the instruments' reentry, the material *is* similar, but sounded remarkably afresh; I understood the sustained textures as the same as before, but the silence had allowed me to prepare my ears for a further acuity in listening. This intensity level existed for some time into the new instrumental material, providing a more heightened, slower temporal flow as I perceived a richer grain in the sonic detail.

Beginning with the silence just over half way through the piece, the sections of silences (regardless of duration, as all are shorter than the first one) seemed to mark duration—or at least, my own journey—through the piece. Because of this, even though they sometimes seemed to divert a progressive temporal course, they would often prompt me to attempt time-ordering processes in recollection; silences like these seem to point both backward and forward, and the more of them I experienced throughout the piece, the more they seemed to challenge me to anticipate, and ready myself for, the next wave of oncoming sustained material.

Compositional methodology

In the final part of this discussion, I want to address the construction methodology which Szlavnics brings to her music. Having broached the piece through a subjective temporal description, followed by a discussion of common individual components as defining their own TG "time-span" (some of which arise from the score, others from the performative action), how might the knowledge of the construction of the piece prompt a review, or reflection, of the temporal experience? How might this reflection affect our disposition toward earlier descriptions?

Szlavnics begins a new piece by making a line drawing on a blank artist's sketchpad. She connects this approach to drawing sound partly due to her some time listening approach to contemporary music of closing her eyes, thus focusing her attention explicitly on the sounds heard, and envisioning related images in her mind. These drawings then seemed to her as some sort of reversal of this process.[14]

This line drawing then has a pitch structure grid superimposed onto it, in which the x-axis is clock duration and the y-axis is pitch height. The y-axis uses a form of just intonation, and for *Gradients of Detail* this is the Extended Helmholtz-Ellis Just Intonation pitch notation, developed by Marc Sabat and Wolfgang von Schweinitz.[15]

The drawing prompted her to trust her own intuitive, organic approach, "calmly and confidently";[16] this approach came from a desire to work outside of what she saw as norms on the contemporary music world at the turn of the twenty-first century, and provided her with a "renewed sense of liberation" at the point of creation of material. Makis Solomos finds a similar organicism in the notational approach, stating that "[t]hese lines are almost like breaths, inscriptions of being: 'I am here, alive, this line proves this. Here is my being in time and space.'" Szlavnics has said that she is concerned about living through the compositional process itself.[17]

She states how she felt her interests necessitated a "notation for a new kind of music," which is "slowed-down (expanded) in order to magnify the audibility of the *detail* of sound"[18]; it is this focus upon the notational approach in her compositional process which elicits such detailed playing by the performers, and thus I believe yields the shifting temporalities in my own listening experience. What may be a series of nonhierarchical shapes in the drawing process (Solomos describes it as "a universe in which everything that exists is of equal importance"[19]), resulted in a complex web of temporalities and shifting flows during my own listening experience.

How does the knowledge that the pitches, intervals, pause durations, and other aspects arise from a line drawing impact upon an exploration of the temporal experience? For one, it reduces (but perhaps not eliminates) the intentionality of the compositional variables such as density/sonority, points at which pauses appear, different speeds of glissandi and other aspects. Thus, I might feel freer still to experience the duration of pauses/glissandi/ and so on without needing to assign clock time (i.e., *count*), or compare the durations of individual pauses with an earlier pause length. Rather, I may simply explore the duration of each pause, experience its duration, without the need to compare; I comprehend it as a pause, a potential silence, which I can experience as any duration (rather than a fixed duration), as a set clock duration has not been specifically chosen for each and every one of these TGs.

Similarly, I may not associate particular harmonies (e.g., the Extended Helmholtz-Ellis Just Intonation major thirds) as marker points within any kind of narrative or journeying structure, but simply as *occurrences*; this necessarily prompts us to experience their duration without priority—they hold no more significance than anything else in this piece—and we don't *wait* upon their sustaining presence, to hear what will follow this significant moment, but rather we glean our own temporal experience from this particular harmony, as opposed to any other harmony. A major-third harmony is different to a close pitch cluster, but in the knowledge that both arise from how close or far away lines happened to be in the original drawing, I find that consequently I apply no further significance to an interval; thus, the temporal experience of, for example, the major third is derived simply from the sonic and associative qualities of that interval subjectively, rather than how it might relate to other harmonic intervals elsewhere in the piece.

While I didn't approach the listening for this chapter through the lens of this compositional methodology, when I reflect upon the focus in my listening commentaries on the changing clusters and densities, and the similarities with the temporal pull of the various gradual glissandi, the method of drawing out these transformations aligns significantly with my listening experience. Perhaps an interesting point here is the highly changeable temporal flow from the different objects and levels of focus which the actualization in performance of the music produces: the glissandi may be notated as clean lines in the notation, but in both Szlavnics' hand-drawn sketches and the changeable detail in the performance of these clean lines, there lies a rich path of nuanced transformations, traces of human action, and a highly variable temporality.

✳ ✳ ✳

Reflecting upon a listening back which focuses on the linear-based construction of the piece, I experienced a heightened perceptual awareness upon a temporality that expands and holds itself up for inspection, as if one were traveling through a sonic hyperspace experiencing these lines extending continuously; the silences, changes in register, bowing changes, and beating patterns are all simply ripples in auditory space-time, occurring one after the other, rich with detail and transformational temporality.

I have steadfastly avoided discussion of clock duration throughout this chapter as I did not set out to describe the specific durational structure of the piece but rather describe my own experiences of temporality and duration. The piece itself is 21:16, and while the listening commentary necessarily provides some indication of the ordering and types of elements employed across the piece's duration, I did not want to focus upon how long different elements lasted, but rather how they impacted my own sense of operating within a temporal flow.

✳ ✳ ✳

The process of analysis of my own temporal response to this music in this chapter has revealed how recollection of earlier material prompts shifts in responses to later gestures, the role silence can play in both memory and temporal flow, and the detail of players' actions embodied in an audio recording can heavily influence my own sense of temporal flow and expansion throughout the listening process.

Szlavnics has developed her own series of questions related to the manner in which music was symbolically represented to her during construction, and how she viewed and handled the material as she prepared it as notation for performers.[20] Similarly, my reflections upon the listening process have directed me to consider further the relationships between the performer and the listener: How can a composer working with notation impact the actioning of an instrument, which produces sound that influences the temporal experience of a listener? In gradual music such as this, do I hear the forms created by the composer, or do I hear the detail in the playing and then deprioritize the memories required to grasp a sense of form?

Gradients of Detail has revealed further to me how I group gradually transforming lines and densities together, how these affect my own sense of temporality, and how silence can help intensify my own attention to these details when they occur. For a piece with such seemingly basic materials at play, the many variables for each parameter described here (such as density in glissando, specific pitch range in register, and bowing actions and beating patterns) show just how nuanced the variation in sonic results, and thus temporal response, can be.

Notes

1   Chiyoko Szlavnics. *Gradients of Detail*, Asasello Quartett, World Edition, WE0022, 2012, compact disc.
2   David Couzens Hoy, *The Time of Our Lives* (Cambridge, MA: MIT Press, 2009), 50.
3   James Tenney, *Meta + Hodos and META Meta + Hodos*, 2nd edn. (Oakland: Frog Peak Music, 1988).
4   James Tenney with Larry Polansky, "Temporal Gestalt Perception in Music," *Journal of Music Theory* 24 no. 2 (1980): 205–241.
5   Brian Belet, "Theoretical and Formal Continuity in James Tenney's Music," *Contemporary Music Review* 27, no. 1 (2008): 26.
6   Ibid., 25.
7   Husserl spoke of a new "primal impression" that corresponds to each new "Now." Hoy, *The Time of Our Lives*, 51.
8   Chiyoko Szlavnics, "Opening Ears: The Intimacy of the Detail of Sound," *Filigrane* 4 (2006), http://www.chiyokoszlavnics.org/texts/details.pdf, 1.
9   Alvin Lucier, *Wind Shadows* (Frankfurt: Material Press, 1994).
10   In *During a Lifetime*, there is a point in which the sinewaves are exposed and create specific polyrhythms; however, the saxophone was introduced to blur the sound in order to avoid the sudden precision. Szlavnics, e-mail to author, August 3, 2017.
11   Chiyoko Szlavnics, "Waves, Ripples, Beats: Psychoacoustic Phenomena Produced by Electronic Means as Compositional Material, and the Potential of Sine Waves to Trace the Acoustical Properties of a Given Room (Heightening

the Listener's Awareness of her/his own Location in it)," presentation, Toronto Electroacoustic Symposium (TES), Toronto, Ontario, Canada, August 10–13, 2011.

12 Szlavnics, e-mail correspondence.

13 Nicolas Collins, Ronald Kuivila, Alvin Lucier, and Michael Roth, *Alvin Lucier: A Celebration* (Middletown: Wesleyan University Press, 2012), 31.

14 Szlavnics, "Opening Ears."

15 See Marc Sabat and Wolfgang Von Schweinitz, "The Extended Helmholtz-Ellis JI Pitch Notation," *Marc Sabat: Music and Writings* (2004), accessed November 19, 2017, http://www.marcsabat.com/pdfs/notation.pdf.

16 Szlavnics, "Opening Ears," 4.

17 Makis Solomos, "Some Preliminary Thoughts on Chiyoko Szlavnics' Music," *Polyphonia* (2015), https://hal.archives-ouvertes.fr/hal-01202895/document.

18 Ibid.

19 Ibid.

20 Szlavnics, "Opening Ears."

Postlude to Chapter Three

Jennie Gottschalk

Chiyoko Szlavnics writes:

> My music requires that the listener step forward, come very close in order to see (hear) the details – just as one would, in order to look at the details of the pigment on a painting. This reflects the actual moment of creation of a work, when I am sitting with my face very close to a page, drawing with a pencil.[1]

Both the translational process of writing *Gradients of Detail* (from a series of drawings to a score) and its form are designed to intensify focus from moment to moment. How then will a more informed listen—at least knowing the prominent types of figures and features likely to occur—inform my experience of the work?

I listened to this piece several years ago and read about it, but I forgot the particular impact and character of its aural events. In my first recent listening, I was aware of its visual genesis and kept thinking of it in terms of shapes. In the second listening, those visual images took something of a back seat to a sense of anticipation, constantly listening forward and imagining what event would occur next. Conversely, Bryn went into the first listening without the same background knowledge, but on his second listen found it hard to switch off the imagery of shapes and tendrils, having read Szlavnics' article.

The methodology of the piece's composition presents a strong suggestion of a quasi-visual mode of listening; but whether in possession of that information or not, other modes are possible. Richard made a conscious decision to avoid such background information in the first part of his chapter, and his attention was drawn to "sudden shifts in listening focus prompted by a heightened *detail* in the sound." For me, the foregrounding and backgrounding of such sonic details is itself relegated to the background through a heightened focus on the imagery evoked by Szlavnics' translational process.

These varied reactions among my own, Bryn's, and Richard's listening experiences underline the fact that the piece transforms itself (more than usual or expected, I would say) according to the questions, memory, and background with which it is approached.

I'll weave the commentary on my second listening together with notes from Bryn's two listenings, Richard's chapter, as well as Szlavnics' essay and some of my own previous and subsequent observations.

At the opening of the piece, harmonic beating creates varying degrees of tension. The degree of tension is the thing in motion, more so than the glissing violins. Bryn speaks of "points of arrival—unisons or chords." The motion toward and arrival at unison correspond at least generally to what I now hear as degrees of tension, which take the foreground. The four instruments are not separate but act as a single organism responding to pressure. This is a visceral impression, and I think it is a direct result of the vibrational impact of the beating patterns. In my first discussion of this piece with Bryn, I remembered this opening as a brief, intense statement. Now it is an unbroken section of over five minutes. Bryn's second listening to this opening seems influenced by Szlavnics' article as well as my reference to degrees of tension: "Tensions, pulling apart, weaving lines, branch-like," and later, "The piece adheres to the principles of tension and release."

The first silence initially feels, to me, like a release. But what returns is a single chord fraught with tension and does not lead to open silences but instead nervous ones. They are full of anticipation of the kinds of chords or tensions that are to come. Bryn has commented that "silences create a strong sense of expectation." Now that I have heard the piece and talked it over, this listening, both in this moment and in other points of transition, is one of anticipation. Silence would seem to be motionless, but the sense of time passing and leading to some new area creates a strong sense of inevitable transition. It is not at all still. A longer silence at 8:00 feels full of possibilities, perhaps because it is longer, and again I find myself surprised by the texture and trajectory of what follows: a swell of harmonic tension that then ebbs to a relative point of stasis.

At 9:27, a sustained tone in one instrument leads into all-instrument activity. Everything is always on the way to something else, whether in instrumentation, harmony, or some other parameter. All silences are anticipatory, sometimes forboding. Richard speaks of these silences as defining temporal gestalts. I hear them more subjectively as opportunities to imagine what comes next. The silences fit within Tenney's idea of the "time after"[2] mentioned in Richard's chapter but are not taken up as events in his listening. He looks more closely at specific sounding elements, rather than the subjective content of the breaks between them.

My anticipations during the silences do not become more accurate as I become more familiar with the piece. While I might try to memorize the sequence of textures, I don't think they would cease to surprise me in their timbral and durational specificity even after several more listenings. This macro form of the piece, its complete unmooring from one texture and launch into another, is consistently disorienting. As Bryn said in our first conversation, "One thing that surprised me was just how multifaceted the experience of listening is." Following his second listening, he commented that he feels as if he is "always in a place that seems unfamiliar, that the musical lines and resultant textures could move anywhere."

The cello pizz at about 11:00 stands out to me as a landmark moment. Every other note up to this point has been sustained, and never short. Another pizz occurs around 14:15. The pizzicati are perhaps so remarkable because they are the only elements of the piece that are not either lines or durations, but simply points. Richard and Bryn also paid special attention to these moments. For Richard they help to define the temporal gestalts, and Bryn calls them "structural markers." They set one thing off from another without being anything other than singular elements.

In the long glissando starting around 19:00, I hear what Bryn meant about equating pitch distance with duration, saying that register "has a direct correspondence with proximity (i.e., a lower note sounds further away because it has further to travel to reach the same goal)." This section does not have the same sense of heightened tension, perhaps because of its lower register. Suddenly the piece is over.

Following the first listening, I remembered this piece as being in many more sections than it was. Perhaps my memory is related to the number of actual silences in the piece, but those are very uneven, both in placement and in duration. They only occasionally correspond to formal sections. The first silence stood out as a prominent demarcator, but subsequent silences got subsumed into the behavior of the piece. The tensions of the piece are related at various times to harmony and beating, register (or literal tension of strings), string noise (which becomes more prominent at less harmonically active moments), silence (anticipation of texture), and speed of motion. I wrote this without meaning to reference Szlavnics' overall comment on the piece, "contrast, register, silence between figures, continuity, non-repetition, and overall form." She doesn't speak specifically of tension here, but the other elements correspond very strongly to Bryn's and my impressions. It is difficult to know exactly how much our listenings were influenced by her writing, but they clearly confirm the success of her intentions.

Notes

1   Chiyoko Szlavnics, "Opening Ears: The Intimacy of the Detail of Sound," *Filigrane* 4 (2006), http://www.chiyokoszlavnics.org/texts/details.pdf, 11.
2   See page 75.

CHAPTER FOUR

Filtering Temporality in Ryoji Ikeda's +/−

Richard Glover

This chapter focuses upon a self-contained set of three tracks from the album *+/−* from 1996. Ikeda's music is produced in the studio, and, as such, this demands for an appropriate response to how it relates to discussion of subjective temporality. Following Jonathan Kramer's emphasis on absolute time (rather than what he terms "experiential time") with regard to electronic music (as he states, "music born of [contemporary] technology demands its own vocabulary and syntax"[1]), these tracks have fixed durations and I have chosen to provide these here:

$$+ \qquad 2:51$$
$$+. \qquad 5:07$$
$$+.. \qquad 10:56$$

These three tracks constitute tracks 4 to 6 on the album, and due to the abstract nature of their titles, they will be referred to as tracks 4, 5, and 6 throughout this chapter.

The *+/−* album was Ikeda's first full album release, and remains his most abstracted exploration into the sculpting and processing of individual sonic pulses. Although later albums such as *Dataplex* (2006), *Test Pattern* (2008), and *Supercodex* (2013) remain firmly in the progressive region between electronica and experimental music, they deploy beat patterns and structures more closely related to the Japanese techno traditions from which

Ikeda emerged in the early 1990s. As such, they deploy broader musical structures and expectation techniques from these fields, prompting less of a close listening to the detail of the sound than those found within +/–, and particularly the three tracks under discussion in this chapter.

The album was part of a number of developing musical tendencies evident in the early 1990s, such as Steve Roden's lowercase movement and the reductionist approach to the music-making of Wandelweiser established by Antoine Beuger and Burkhard Schlothauer in 1992. Ikeda was part of a movement of Japanese electronica artists deriving from a post-techno, post-digital scene captivated by the potential of digital technology to explore the phenomenology of sound and time. He told David Toop that he felt the most important aspect of the album +/– was the relationship between the perception of the listener and the physiological effects of the music[2]; this focus upon immediacy of sound and vibration, sound and signal, is explored throughout +/– and provides highly unique listening experiences.

The reasons for focusing on just these three tracks from what is a ten-track album are for the support of a clarity in documentation of experience. These three tracks (which I will refer to as the + tracks) are of a type, in terms of the sound worlds they inhabit, and their broader creative approaches. The album can effectively be split up into four sections, including the + tracks (appearing as tracks 4 through 6 on the album), the three tracks preceding them (Headphonics 0/0, 0/1, and 1/0), the three tracks succeeding them (-, -., and -..), and a final coda-like track +/–. Tracks 1 through 3 explore sine tones, white noise and quick pulses which almost bleed into a single-sustained tone, tracks 7 through 9 utilize sine tones to explore divergent lines and beating patterns,[3] and track 10—at only 1:05 in duration—consists solely of ultra-high sine tones right on the horizon of the human hearing range. The scope of different experiences across these three sets of three tracks (excluding the final track) is so varied that to set out to explore them all in one chapter would run counter to the argument which this book aims to communicate: that by focusing in high-level detail on individual temporal experiences, rather than more generalized descriptions which necessarily compromise on detail, much can be revealed about the nature of subjectivity and temporal experiences in response to these radical musical listening scenarios.

While a focus upon any of the sets of three tracks would have undoubtedly yielded a rich exploration of my own perception, understanding, and experiential processes in listening, I selected +, +., and +.. (tracks 4 through 6 on the album) in particular due to the contrast they exhibit in sonic material to the previous chapter on Szlavnics' *Gradients of Detail* as a result of their rhythmic intensity, that thus prompt significantly different temporal experiences in response to my listening. The contrast in duration between the first of the set (track 4) and the final track (over three times the duration) also suggested a particularly unique aspect: How would my listening evolve, across increasingly lengthening tracks, at such a large rate of expansion (ratios of 1.7 : 3.1 : 6.6, rounded up)? I wanted to explore how a sense of preparation and accustomization might occur throughout the tracks, and how that would impact upon my own temporal awareness.

However, the chapter attempts to uncover as much about the difference *between* the + tracks—related to their ordering, speed of the pulse, overall duration, and other aspects—than just the nature of the minimal sonic environment employed overall by the three tracks. Again, this chapter maintains the overall arguments of the book that to discuss temporal experience, and thus to discuss subjectivity, is to discuss and explore the *specific*, rather than the generalizable. While I do make claims relating to the three tracks as a grouping in comparison to other specific pieces toward the end of the chapter, these claims are made in the shadow of the specificity of the discussions for each individual track.

Methodology

While the text retains an emphasis upon the specific, it is not the job of this chapter to detail every single sonic transformation which occurs throughout these three tracks. Therefore, with this chapter I have not provided a commentary to—or documentation of—an individual listening, but rather the chapter as a whole is an accumulation of the experiences gained from all listenings; I do not attempt to recreate the sonic environment or transformations across the + tracks, but instead reference particular sonic aspects of the music where appropriate to elucidate the exploration of temporal experience.

As the pieces are of shorter duration, my listening methodology has been quite different to that employed with the Szlavnics. I have listened numerous times to the tracks individually, but I based this chapter specifically around my experiences of listening to the three tracks in a single sitting, one track after another, in the order which they appear on +/– in order to explore the impact of each new track upon memory and developments in my perceptual mechanisms.

The chapter will similarly address the three tracks in broad sequential order with an emphasis upon the first track to address the experience of listening to such minimal material, although as stated certain elements which are shared across the tracks will be referred to throughout. Discussion of how the listening experience of each new track is impacted by what is heard previously will then be brought in as appropriate. Although the writing in the chapter may suggest a linearity in my listening experience of these tracks, and thus in my reflection, I do not intend for this to be communicated from the structure. A spider diagram, or virtual 3D space, would communicate more accurately the nonlinearity of my own experiences from this music, including the entanglement of reflections following the listenings.

The focus of the chapter is the experience of the sound itself; a discussion of the technology used in the production would lie outside of my own subjective temporal experience and focus upon the processes of construction of the music. The three tracks are certainly a marker of technology in the mid-1990s, but this chapter focuses as much as is possible on my own subjective response to temporalities *as experienced*, and to discuss these as a distinct topic for examination.

✳ ✳ ✳

Track 4 (the first track of the set) begins with a sonic gesture that underpins much of the material of the three tracks: an extended filter sweep, which here moves me gradually from initial high frequencies on the horizon of audibility, through to a more rounded timbre; this sweep operates upon a continuous fast pulse and gradually leads to a clearer perception of the timbre of the pulse throughout the duration of the sweep.

Once my listening is attuned to the filter sweeps, I begin to perceive this gesture—or at least, the impact of the gesture—occurring often, regardless of whether it is actually present in the auditory material or not; I become aware that my mind is creating auditory hallucinations. My perceptual focus has been one of *following* the shape of the sweeps, thus temporal experience has been driven by gradual, predictable transformation. I am caught in that following of the curve, which dictates a steady, unchanging temporal flow and in which the continuous pulse actually recedes within my broader perceptual focus, which is dominated by the gradual sweeps. It seems as if I am being encouraged to explore the spectral range through the gradual change, and the continuous pulse is a mechanism, a tool, to allow me to do that. There are echoes of Larry Polansky describing James Tenney's music as "providing a tool to help you evolve"[4]—my ability to focus perceptual mechanisms seems to enhance while applying my attention to this track.

Here, I feel as if I am continually pushed forward, to anticipate how a particular timbral shape will be revealed. The gradual sweeps afford me a clear ability to anticipate, and during the sections where no apparent sonic transformation has been applied to the pulse, I am somewhat in a state of anticipation for what the next transformation will be. I seem to superimpose my own spectral transformations upon the pulse; I sense that there is little, if any, change in the perceived auditory material (i.e., the pulses), but nonetheless my active perceptual mechanisms create filter sweeps over different durations and frequency ranges. My perception seems to struggle with auditory stability, and thus temporality seems to slow down somewhat, as the detail of these imagined spectral changes are "perceived."

Then, with sudden clarity, I distinguish a gradual filter sweep existing within the track itself, as opposed to my own perception. I aim to track the higher pitch curve of this change (as the sweep occurs over discrete pulses, it is an example of good continuation, in that we fuse the frequential changes together to envisage it as a continuous, "joined up" curve moving through the frequency spectrum over time), which prompts a move *away* from temporal awareness during these slow gestures, and toward the changing pitch curve itself—and particularly toward the anticipation of the teleological endpoint of that spectral change. This shift of awareness away from my own temporal experience and toward pitch/melodic activity shows similarities with the experience of the glissandi in Szlavnics' *Gradients of Detail*; in these shifts between unchanging pulses and gradual filter sweeps, it is as if I am being wrenched out of a landscape which I populate with my own imagination, and into one being populated by an external force.

There are similarities to Jonathan Kramer's nondirected linearity here,[5] in which a sense of linearity operates at foreground levels within the sonic environment but without a directionality built into the underlying structure. Ikeda's filter sweeps with their inherent gestural directedness do not seem to lead toward a final sense of closure; however, within each sweep there is a clear localized directionality—indeed, these provide moments for my listening to focus upon and increase the rate of the temporal flow.

Similarly to the wrenching from one landscape to another, the sudden shifts in contrasting spectra which occur from roughly halfway through track 4 move me from a very free-flowing listening mode in which I seemed to impose my own spectral change upon the sound, and into a very constrained sonic environment; each time there is a shift, my *awareness* of my creative temporal perception is heightened, before my perception then becomes restricted by the material following the shift. In contrast, where these new environments are sustained, the creative imagination begins again.

However, the presence of the continuous pulse is a disruptive force toward this fluidity of the simple perception of the melodic curve produced by the spectral change, either real or imagined. Alongside hearing timbral change, my perception is continually striving to generate rhythmic patterns from within this pulse. There is a different form of continual creativity in my perceptual mechanisms here, distinct from when I impose my own filter sweeps upon the pulse, as the rate and short duration of the consistent pulses fairly quickly brings into question my own ability to perceive rhythmic consistency, and my neural processing seems to refute the possibility of the pulse rate remaining entirely stable. I unwittingly parse the continual flow of pulse attacks, occasionally detecting dotted or swung rhythms, even though I am aware that they do not exist. By attempting to chunk these sections, my perceptual sense is trying to form a grammar, a syntax, from the continuous flow. It is only when changes from a gradual spectral envelope occur that I become aware that my perceptual senses are less concerned with trying to find contrasting rhythmic patterns—and thus parsing up the continuous flow—and rather attempting to detect any kind of timbral differentiation. Even with this knowledge, however, I still inevitably attempt to parse out rhythms in future sections of the track over stable pulses.

I certainly experience disoriented moments in which I am unsure what aspects are changing and when they are remaining constant. I sense I am finding it difficult to perceive distinction in the sound, and as such I accept absolute continuity, which itself shifts the temporal experience to a more detailed, considered, compressed environment; even in the moments when I do perceive stability in the sound, my perception seems to be drawn toward a movement which might not even be there. This track seems to be prompting my imagination as much as anything else, and thus temporality slows down when I anticipate, or imagine, change.

The fast-paced pulse continues unabated throughout, and this relentlessness seems to somehow prompt a detailed attention upon each pulse, even though I know the pulse is too fast for me to actually perceive each attack—yet I still feel its impact. What seems interesting to me is that the fast pace does not yield a smooth, rapid movement of temporal flow in synchronization with the pulse. Rather, it seems to underpin temporal transformations due to my imagined timbral changes, stemming from a closer listening to each pulse than I might perform if the pulse rate were a certain amount slower.

One of the more difficult experiential issues in this track was the ability of my long-term memory to differentiate between similar gestures, most prominently the gradual filter sweeps, especially when they all followed similar arcs and durations. This causes significant issues in cognitive processing, behind attempting to understand what relationship there exists between events as part of a larger construction, when particular orderings cannot be comprehended due to the inherent similarity between these gestures. The pulses provide the foundations for these sweeps, and so they cannot effectively be understood as marker points to differentiate; similarly the filter sweeps, and occasional sudden shifts in the timbre of the pulsations, do not provide significant enough contrasts for them to be individually distinguished, and thus an underlying pattern or structure proves exceptionally difficult to determine. Bob Snyder states that "it is much easier to build up a representation in memory of music that exhibits clear groupings and closures than of music that does not,"[6] which aligns with these observations.

The changes in track 4 are almost too similar to reflect upon (indeed, this is only heightened in the two subsequent tracks, with their longer durations and many more gradual sweeps); it is almost impossible to retain in my short-term memory the kinds of textural and spectral sound worlds which have already been sounded, and there were few clear groupings to be made. In recollection, these groupings were not distinct enough to be placed within any kind of time-ordering. The continuity of the pulse and its changing detail (either within the material or shaped within my imagination) were the overriding memories carried through.

I cannot determine any sense of linearity from one spectral sweep or sudden shift to the next; there seems to be no "default" state to the pulse. I haven't heard a significant sonority from which other gestures, or timbres, relate or derive. Each section of relative stability in the perceived lack of transformation (aside from a highly focused listening which seems to superimpose spectral change onto consistency of timbre) adopts a sort of reference, but only during its existence; once a new spectral sweep is initiated, I usually lose a clear sense of the previous state of stability, and instead focus attention upon the potential destination point of this new transformation.

If memory is consciousness of the past,[7] then these tracks raise an intense awareness of one's own consciousness of what occurred previously. What am I able to recollect? I know that I experienced difficulty in parsing the sonic stream, but I also know that I had awareness of the global sound world; at any one point, I would consider how much the *remembered* sound world was different to what I am now experiencing, and whether I am experiencing something different to before (except that I am now experiencing it in *this* present). The very gradual increase of lower frequencies in track 4 is only perceivable on reflection, somewhere toward the end of the track; there is very little opportunity to perceive this change actually occurring, thus very precisely setting up a temporality in which my recall facilities are narrowed, limited. Following this revelatory ability to reflect upon the global timbral change in the track, Ikeda then effectively presents the sonic material from the beginning and end of the track; I heard the very high frequential band with a little bass for a short duration at 2:08, and then a shift to the mid-heavy sound at 2:22, as if to confirm this transformation. The durations of these are experienced as fairly short, matching clock durations, but what they provide is an opportunity—or rather a further muddying of resonances—to attempt to re-experience the present from both the beginning and the end of the global transformation. This necessarily proves futile—again, the lack of ability to parse any distinct gesture, phrase, duration, from earlier in the track means that it is recollected as one extended stream, and thus, there is only an estimation that these sonic signatures occurred within the track, at very different structural moments.

Track 4, with its extended filter sweeps through high frequency, seems to prepare me for the quicker timbral contrasts which appear in track 5. However, my perception cannot maintain such a close, intense focus upon these quicker sweeps and higher rate of timbral shifts, and I feel I am impelled to change focal levels from what I thought I would require from track 4.

This second track of the set of three is over twice as long as the first, and following an initial short section of stability in the auditory material which actually provides a stable temporal flow, becomes more sectional, and thus less difficult to parse—although most certainly no less straightforward to recall and identify time-ordering. This conflict of clear timbral contrast between the two different tracks and constituent sections within them, and the insistent, relentless unchanging pulse of each track, results in distinctly difficult time-ordering capabilities. The continuous pulse seems to hamper any perceptual attempt to recall sections and arrange them in memory, and instead the pulse prompts me to retain perceptual attention upon the present sounding environment. It seems like it is only when the contrasting sections in the track are introduced, following the initial relative timbral stability, that the track begins to fill in the tapestry of the temporal experience; what was a relatively clean, almost comprehendible, space is crowded with instability, unreliability, and disorientation.

How much of these disorientation experiences can I, or should I, attribute to Ikeda's own creative capacities? I didn't feel like I was being forced into any specific experience by the human who created these tracks, but rather that person was creating an environment which they knew would prompt significant changes, disruptions, in any listener's experience—without knowing exactly how those experiences would manifest themselves. It would be easy for me to attribute all experiences as responding to a carefully calculated plan, but of course any creator cannot know, or guarantee, the response from any particular listener. While a medium such as electronic music can allow a closer connection to be made between author and listener as compared to musics in which performer-interpreters are involved in consciously shaping the auditory experience, in my own listening experiences of these tracks I have not felt pushed, or controlled, by Ikeda but rather felt free to attempt to investigate and understand my own temporal experiences, in the knowledge that the sonic environment will prompt heightened awareness and introspection. My awareness of what I am terming the creativity in my perceptual mechanisms reveals to me how much of my *own* input determines my experience here.

Because of this heightened state of awareness, I sense the minimal material in the music has primed my listening, so that by track 5 I am able to detect nuances much more clearly, and indeed to the point that certain changes seem like sensory overload; how do I compensate my close listening with these suddenly ferocious changes? The temporal experience widens, broadens, as these large-scale changes (i.e., within the reference of the track) take considerable cognitive processing to adjust. Any attempt at positioning these changes within the time-ordering of the track is particularly difficult, due to the maximal contrast seeming to be far more significant, and capable of being differentiated, than much previous sonic material.

This provides an interesting contrast with Szlavnics' *Gradients of Detail*, in which slow gradual textural change affords an ability to compare and contrast with previous sections, and I can attempt to build up a sequence of events, or at the least smaller sublevel sequences of events. This inability in these first two Ikeda tracks to easily arrange what I perceived as discrete sections due to contrasting spectral envelopes means that the sound seems to pass by me—I almost perceive the temporal flow passing in front or around me—without my being able to keep up and cognitively process the sonic signals I am receiving.

There is a point in track 5 where the pulse has an emphasis added to every alternate beat, and I immediately begin to parse the pulse flow into on- and offbeats. However, my own perception is continually switching the dominant on-beat between different pulses, and therefore there is no consistency for me to fall back into, and the temporal flow remains utterly in flux: a continual shifting, unsecured temporality suddenly hastening, suddenly relaxing, without a balance or reliability.

Of all three tracks, track 5 has the most disjointed contrasts; halfway through there is much variation, which eventually leads into a sequence of continued contrasting emphases of different frequency bands on almost every pulse. This section develops its own grammar—one which has not been anticipated beforehand in this track, or in track 4; following the sustained filter sweeps of previous material, this sudden, highly contrasting language changes too quickly for me to process—at once I am being quickly pulled through a temporal vortex, and standing outside viewing in without processing detail.

The return to the gestural sweeps at the end of the track, as well as being more detailed than the beginning, necessarily now feels much more temporally uneven and detailed, following the amount and variety of disjointed emphases heard previously. I have been enabled to chunk distinct gestures, which I can now perceive as different enough due to their temporal proximity to each other within the track; sweeps are shorter, and bleed into one another. I am caught up with this interplay: the force of the pulse recedes into the background, and temporal awareness ebbs away with it, to be usurped by the interplay and discourse between filter-gestures.

As my listening methodology was centered around hearing all three tracks in the order they appear on the album, I also experienced the manner in which Ikeda conceived how the listener would encounter the transition of one track to the next. Tracks 5 and 6 also include a much more pronounced use of noise at the very beginning of each track (much more so than the click found at, for instance, the beginning of track 8 of the album), and these sudden gestures create a unique impact upon my focus on the temporal flow across the three tracks.

The two different noise disruptions occurring at the beginning of tracks 4 and 5 consist of almost a second's worth of sine and sawtooth tones, different color noises and other clicks and electronically generated sounds, which serve to interfere with any kind of listening habits built up by the end of the previous track, as if to disconnect the oncoming track with what has been heard previously. They are both sudden, as no parametric change has created any expectation of either track 4 or 5 ending, and their high contrast in sonic material with the slow filter sweeps of the pulse, which are the only sounds I was exposed to by this point (in this set of the album) ensures that they stand out quite significantly and interfere with perceptual experience from one track to the next. While they don't erase memories or listening habits from previous tracks, there is an impact, a brief stage wipe of memories in the perceptual present.

In track 6, this disruption is followed by sixteen clicks of the pulse at a speed of what is consequently revealed as being four times as slow as the main pulse in the rest of the track. I had by this point comprehended the sonic disruption as introducing a new track, but the slower pulse engenders a quite startling, if only brief, unique temporal experience: the contrast between the previous quicker pulses from previous tracks (which the sonic disruptions have interfered with, but by no means erased from memory) gives a much wider, expansive temporal field, as if this track will cover much broader gestures, more varied sonic environments, and move away significantly from what has been heard on tracks 4 and 5. However, the introduction of the much quicker pulse after sixteen of these slower-paced clicks returns me back to a listening mode similar to that of the previous tracks; the sudden changes of temporal environment at the beginning of this track, from the sonic disruption, to the slow clicks, to the faster pulse, constitute the most intense variations in my temporality as experienced across the set of the three tracks. This immediately places my listening mode in a more animated state—supported by the quicker pulse of the track—and thus my own temporal flow is spinning, uncontrolled, off-kilter almost, from the beginning of the track. Anticipation becomes problematic, and, despite the now-experienced continuity of the pulse, I sense a temporal environment which could expand or contract violently. Again, I feel as though my listening approaches are being prepared so as to experience the possible considerable temporal variation presented by the rest of this final track of the set.

As Ikeda increases the pulse rate across each of the three tracks, this counteracts my perceptual system's tendency to gradually relinquish primary focus upon the continual pulse. Having heard the slower pulse rates of the previous two tracks, the quicker rate of this track makes it seem more transformative, and more that the potential for more change, movement, development is possible. However, the filter sweeps beginning from just over half a minute into the track tend to act on a more glacial timescale in track 6 which creates a cavernous contrast with track 5. The initial emphasis and dynamism of the quicker pulse renders this slower timbral transformation in much more defined, lucid detail, giving these extended sweeps their own nature, or character. This causes the movement into an exploration of the higher-frequency bands to become much more heightened, and I experience this section as having an intensified temporal flow compared to much of the track beforehand, a temporal experience which makes me more aware of sweep duration, and the push/pull of flow as a linear frequency sweep plays itself out. With such a limited palate of sonic material due to the more extended durations of the filter sweeps, I seem to only experience more and more intensified temporal flows in this final track of the set.

From 6:30, this track contains echoes of track 5's highly contrasting sequence of frequency band emphases. However, I find it hard to determine how many of these similarities are contained with the audio I am perceiving, and how many I am superimposing onto what may be stable, frequentially unchanging material, in a very similar manner to earlier tracks but this time reinforced by the possibility of Ikeda intentionally referring to the heightened timbral alteration from the second half of track 5. The experience of disorientation which occurs from this seems to only be supported—if not encouraged—by the again relentless pulse; there is no opportunity to reflect upon my experience here, no real chance to recall shapes, speeds, and contrasts. I seem to be listening to music which heavily prompts me to experience, and remain aware of, the present.

The pulse rate in this final track lies on the horizon of my ability to chunk out separate sections, patterns, or gestures. At many moments in this track, I began to sense a continuous stream of sound with constant emphases, rather than discrete individual pulses. I begin to occasionally listen for pitch diversions, wondering whether phenomena from layered sustained tones such as the beating patterns appearing in the Szlavnics are occurring— which with reflection seems highly unlikely in a track consisting entirely of individual pulses; but the effect of this searching in my listening approach certainly impacted upon my temporal experience. As with the change of pulse rate at the beginning of the track, these transitions of listening modes seemed to widen out the temporality I existed in, to invite an exploration of the sound—until a new filter sweep then assumed the focus of my listening attention, and the pulses-as-continuous-stream listening mode ebbed away.

At 7:15, I begin to perceive a high melody, which coheres together in my perception, rather than remaining as a series of separate pulses which it must be as it is clearly constructed from harmonics of the pulses. I seem to perceive more melodic movement, and again—similar to the end of track 5—I follow that line. I become aware that my shifts of focus in this piece revolve largely around my cognitive functions *processing* the onslaught of pulses, and being led either by the sweeps or particularly by what I perceive as melodic movement in the high harmonics. The extraordinary difference between this latter material, with line, shape, and *journey*, compared with the stability of the unchanging pulses, is foregrounded heavily due to the limited range of auditory material experienced throughout the three tracks. The line itself seems to wander, with no real destination or sense of anticipation apparent. It becomes clear very quickly that it is a product of boosting particular high harmonics; this contrasts heavily with the spectral sweeps, which have a high level of predictability about them, even if I as a listener do not know their destination point. In reflecting upon these experiences, I understand that I follow the spectral sweeps by a sense of being *led*, whereas the brief melodic lines I explore with more of a sense of *curiosity*, in which I understand that this melodic line will not lead me to a different sound world, or developed state from where I am at the point of listening.

There is a gradual ebb and flow of temporal experience throughout track 6; the distinct shift in the middle of the track to a more bass-dominated timbre doesn't alter that ebb and flow, but it is only upon a clear return to the full frequency shape of the pulse that this becomes one of the few moments of certainty of recollection—which heightens this experience of an ebb and flow, a sporadic crunching together of the temporal flow.

Upon repeated listenings, I do not consciously attempt to recreate or understand a simplified structural rendition of the track. It wouldn't serve to underscore my own experiences when listening to the track, regardless of what patterns or relationships I might find; the continuity of the pulse, like the two staves on the bottom of the page across the entirety of Cardew's *Treatise* (1963–67), suggest a platform for which other aspects are conveyed, transformed, described, prompted; but to look within those materials for structural relationships is a red herring. I feel the need to persist in examining only my listening experience, rather than referring to outside sources or referents such as any structural references I might make. Filter sweeps and frequency band shifts occur, but they do not preempt or engender new sound worlds or materials.

Toward the end of this track, the high-mids of the frequency range create a highly intensified sound which seems to prompt even further lilting rhythms from the continuous pulse; the piercing sound leaves virtually no trace of transformation from sweeping, and thus my focus again switches toward the stability of the pulse. It is an exceptionally revealing listening experience as the pulse again seems to parse into discrete rhythms, and at other points seems to simply increase and decrease in tempo, forever shifting and providing very little ability to recollect particular events experienced previously in the track.

The silence at the end of track 6 is really the only silence experienced in the entirety of these three tracks. It is sudden—as with the earlier tracks, no parametric change toward the end of the track engenders any sense of anticipation, and repeated listenings do very little (if anything at all) to prepare me for the moment when this silence appears, and to lessen the impact of it upon my experience. Where a clear expectation of closure (e.g., a speeding up/slowing down of the pulse and an increase/decrease in dynamics) enables a listener to prepare for reflection and initiate recollection of previous moments and perceived responses, the extreme-ness of the sudden silence after 10:45 of very fast pulses provides almost no anticipated platform for reflection, recollection, or awareness of temporal experience. The sudden *lack* of high-intensity pulses resulted for me in more of an auditory blinking in the daylight, in which I was only able to adjust to this new environment of silence which I had not realized had been so distant to my experience throughout the three tracks. My ears adjust by seemingly reducing their irises, and my cognitive listening processes can only attempt to experience, rather than interpret or reflect upon, this silence—and certainly not consider and compare previous material. The silence is at the end of the set of the seemingly continuous sound world of the tracks, yet it is also *the* end of it, as my own temporal experience during this silence forms an extraordinary conclusion to the listening experience. I sensed that this silence is here to provide the listener with a platform to conclude their listening experience themselves; as recollection and time-ordering proved so difficult for me here, I experienced the force of that silence as much as the sonic material in the rest of the track.

Comparison with other pieces

In order to contextualize my listening experience of the high-intensity pulse flows in these tracks, I want to draw upon some other works which are centered around a consistent pulse throughout.

There are highly contrasting temporal experiences within, for instance, the repetitive onsets over sustained durations of Steve Reich's *Drumming* (1970–71) or Glenn Branca's *Symphony No. 1* (1981); however, the speed of the pulse in these Ikeda tracks, the continuity of dynamic, the exploration of the spectral range, and the lack of any additional elements are such that I have a much more heightened sense of awareness of the pulse than in these other works. While there are plenty of other pieces demanding a focused, localized listening which contain sections of fast pulse rates, few base their entire concept around a structure entirely of continuity in pulse.

When I listen to the repetitive guitar pulsing of Branca's *Symphony No.1*, I notice the different onsets made by the many different players and the difference in dynamic weighting between individual strums, percussive hits, which push a focus toward the human actioning of those sounds; I consider the collective actions of music-making involved, the coordination necessary to bring about this synchronization of note onset, and then conversely the differences inherent within this broader level of synchronization which are brought about by the many different performative agents at work. Indeed, this web of note onsets for each pulse is a significant part of the concept of the piece, and this temporal awareness, while still heightened here, is impacted upon by performer actions.

Similarly, the continuity of pulse in Reich's *Drumming*—for instance, the marimbas of Part II—provides a significantly different temporal flow than the Ikeda, due to the emphasis on rhythmic pattern, superimposed upon the pulse. The pulse rate is very fast here, as in the Ikeda, but the changing rhythmic patterns are the focus. There are many moments in *Drumming* where there are rests, giving sustained rhythmic patterns prominence over a section; this does not occur in the Ikeda due to the absolute consistency in dynamic and pulse rate throughout each track.

While there are parallels between the changing rhythmic emphases and the filter sweeps of Ikeda's electronic pulses, what I felt distinguishes the Ikeda is the lack of teleological motion across these three tracks. Across much of *Drumming*, there are clear local-level processes which direct rhythmic patterns to merge one into another; there is a specific sequential order to these transformations, with the particular goal of prompting emergent patterns to be audibly perceived. The temporal experience is underpinned by the sense of teleological flow, in which one anticipates each new emergent pattern, understanding its relationship to material as having been generated as a result of processes *upon* that material. While there is a continual pulse, Ikeda's sweeps and timbral shifts do not follow in a linear, logical form, but rather seemingly as ways to use the rate of the pulse to heighten attention toward a temporal flow. *Drumming*'s pulse highlights the emergent patterns, and—as with the Branca—is noticeably slower, prompting my attention much more toward a narrative arising from the various rhythmic emphases and emergent patterns, along with broader issues of ensemble interaction and synchronicity.

In Philip Glass' *Music in Similar Motion*, my perceptual focus lies firmly within the melodic development of the music; the additive and subtractive processes push me to anticipate melodic direction, note choice, intervallic relationships, and to consider future melodic development, rather than decide to focus—or rather, undergo the requisite shift in focus—for appreciating the percussive, persistent nature of Ikeda's pulses and their impact upon the transitions in my own temporal experience. To me, there is no sense when listening to the Ikeda of loops, of return, or repetition; I only experienced a temporality of unfolding, of a continual rush through new territory rather than cycling through patterns or a linear transformation of process. The melodic movement found in the contours of the filter sweeps in Ikeda's music does not progress in such a rationalized, predictable manner as with the Glass, and as such the note onsets are heard more as melodic extensions, rather than as percussive pulse with timbral transformation which I sensed much more in the Ikeda.

Perhaps more importantly, though, the pulse rate of even the slowest of the Ikeda tracks (track 4) at 584 bpm is still much faster than these ensemble pieces mentioned; the ferocity of this tempo, combined with extremely short durations of the pulses (emphasized by the entire lack of any resonance from the sound) ensures that the + tracks prompt an entirely unique listening when heard alongside other works deriving from minimal approaches to unchanging tempi.

While there are also many musics involving a relentless high-tempo percussive line such as those found in the techno and progressive dance worlds from which Ikeda comes, as this chapter focuses upon close listening to this music through both speakers and headphones, musics which are first and foremost designed to be heard and moved to in large venues have been considered outside of the scope of the discussion. Research in entrainment within musics demonstrate the manner in which bodies respond to music through movement,[8] but this chapter—and book—has as its central theme the response to the mind's temporal experiences from listening in detail, in quiet listening conditions, to allow examination of transformations in listening modes and corresponding temporalities as felt. Similarly, electronic musics which may demand close listenings, such as progressive electronica artists like Carsten Nicolai and Mark Fell, while featuring sections of fast-paced pulsed music derived from dance music patterns, rarely create tracks entirely from a continuous pulse, unchanging in its dynamic (aside from dynamic changes as a result of timbral transformation) and speed. Often these sections are juxtaposed alongside sections of other, contrasting material, to form a narrative to a track, rather than the pulses forming the consistent element, and primary focus, of any one track.

Speakers and headphones

In considering tracks with such nuanced production as these, one major variable which impacts upon one's own temporal sense is the mode of listening; here I want to explore the difference in two different listening situations which I employed for this chapter—using loudspeakers within a closed-room setting, and listening through headphones—in order to discuss the impact which these different modes can have upon temporal experiences. While this chapter cannot accommodate for all of the variations of these media (different room sizes and building materials, speaker types, speaker models and arrangements, headphone types, etc.), I will be discussing and comparing the different experiences from listening through speakers, and through headphones, in order to further question what impacts temporal flow, and why might these results occur.

For these three tracks, headphones provide a highly contrasting, intensified experience; I hear far more high frequencies in the sound, and am thus able to detect more nuanced control in production. The sweeps seem more detailed, and I find that I follow the contour of the sweeps in an even closer focus than when listening through speakers. There is also more of an immediate response to the intensity of the pulses, and I impose my own slight spectral variation upon the pulses as I listen more closely, becoming aware that I am consciously carrying out this process.

However, when listening to the tracks through speakers, I can change the directionality of my head which enables me to control the high frequencies I perceive. Listening while wearing headphones, on the other hand, necessarily makes this task all but impossible—I am forced to focus upon the frequencies being directed straight into my ears, rather than having control over the directionality of my own auditory apparatus. While awareness of this only becomes clearer upon repeated listening across both modes, it impacted upon my temporal experiences in that I felt that a certain loss of control over my abilities to create my own structured listening response to the music; there was a much stronger sense of being pulled along by the temporal flow of the fast pulse rate when listening with headphones, as opposed to the more open sonic environment created by speakers which allowed me to shape and explore the landscape of the filter sweeps, for instance, which enabled a greater sensation of the perceptual present, and being able to broaden out my own position within a temporal flow.

When listening with headphones, I am directed toward focusing upon the differentiated high harmonic line captured toward the end of track 5 which is not as pronounced as when heard through speakers. This introduction of an individual line acting seemingly separate to the pulses lies in stark contrast to the continual *sonority* of the pulses, focusing upon the timbral change rather than the character and development of individual lines. As I continue to listen to this distinct compositional device, it draws me away from the listening modes I had employed while following the relentlessness of the pulse. There is a renewed focus upon *line*; my perception moves away from pulse rate, the consistency of that pulse, and gradual change, and moves toward something which could be described as *voice*. My temporal experience transforms distinctly, as I experience a changeable flow which I cannot anticipate in terms of melodic direction or gesture, as opposed to the predictability inherent in the continuous pulse.

The self-contained nature of the audio tracks is evident: there is no sense of expanse, and there are very clearly no environmental or studio effects added to imply a sense of space within which to position the sound. However, when listening through speakers, those environments situate themselves within the acoustic of the room or space; while any listening of the tracks necessarily undergoes this process, the specific reverb-free sound world of Ikeda's tracks transforms into a sonic object in space, when compared to the listening experience through headphones.

While Ikeda makes use of the stereo space, the sound is not designed to develop within a clearly communicated acoustic, which in itself draws attention toward the timbral envelope and the gestural qualities of the sound itself, rather than its impact upon a virtual space and therefore its external situation. The dry sonic materials of short pulses, requiring a near-silence in any listening environment for them to be clearly audible, prime my ears for close listening rather than any form of more global, structure-oriented listening. Were this music to somehow be performed on any kind of acoustic instruments, the focus would quickly shift to the endurance capacity of the performers and their ability to maintain an absolute continuity in aspects such as pulse rate, dynamic, duration, and so on. As it is, the sound— without any seeming intentional external associations—is presented as being situated nowhere except in the listener's mind, to be explored as itself, with all experiences which that listener brings.

Concluding comments

This set of three tracks, when listened to sequentially, prompt very specific patterns of listening modes, and thus the range of temporal experiences feels fairly restrained, restricted; there is no sense that a broad range of temporalities have been explored, as with the Szlavnics, but rather the tracks—with their tight focus upon the spectral transformation of a continuous, stable pulse which is often perceived as varying—yields a narrow band of temporal experiences. However, this narrow band is magnified more and more over the three tracks, such that at certain moments these smaller shifts are experienced as momentous transitions.

In my reflections upon these experiences, I focus much more on the difference between the stability in the pulse rate, and my own perceived instability of that rate. While I understand that the rate is not changing, I found it almost impossible not to perceive change, and thus any temporal flow was continually shifting, extending, and contracting as per my own perceptual system's attempts to vary, differentiate, and distinguish the sonic material. To make an analogy with sustained tone music in which an electronic held tone sustains the exact same frequency throughout, I often begin to imagine that I perceive frequency drift within the tone, where none may actually be sounding.

There exists an experientially rich discord between the low-information incoming perceptual stream of consistency and the continual emphasis upon different pulses and patterns which my perceptual system superimposes, which prompts multiple and frequent deviations in temporal flow, even within the narrow band of temporal experience mentioned above. It is as if Ikeda is testing my perceptual abilities across the three tracks, utilizing a reduced language of timbral manipulation and graduated pulse-rate changes between the tracks to implement that examination. Ikeda's high pulse rate throughout the + tracks ensures the gestural sweeps and timbral shifts provide highly localized teleologies, and engenders a greatly heightened awareness of the transformational nature of the temporal flow.

Much earlier in this chapter I discussed how my early familiarizations with these tracks led me to conclude that the pulses were present only to serve the filter sweeps, timbral shifts, and the broader exploration of frequential emphasis and sculpting which Ikeda employs; after my full consideration of what impacts upon my temporal experiences throughout these tracks, it seems very much that this perceptual loop is closed, as ultimately I consider that these gradual and sudden frequential gestures serve only to bring about awareness of the speed, intensity, and relentlessness of the pulse rate across the tracks.

Notes

1   Jonathan D. Kramer, *The Time of Music* (New York: Schirmer, 1988), 72.
2   David Toop, *Haunted Weather* (London: Serpent's Tail, 2005), 12.
3   And also follow the structural pattern of tracks 4–6 in which each track in a set of three is longer than the last, with track 7 at 6:37, track 8 at 11:52, and track 9 at 13:25; the ratio of these durations is quite different to the + tracks.
4   Larry Polansky, "Jim Tenney and Space Travel," *Perspectives of New Music* 25, no. 1 (1987): 437–438.
5   Kramer, *Time of Music*, 39–40.
6   Bob Snyder, *Music and Memory* (Cambridge, MA: MIT Press, 2001), 66.
7   David Couzens Hoy, *The Time of Our Lives* (Cambridge, MA: MIT Press, 2009), 101.
8   See Martin Clayton "What is Entrainment? Definitions and Applications in Musical Research," *Empirical Musicology Review* 7, nos. 1–2 (2012): 49–56.

Postlude to Chapter Four

Bryn Harrison

The three tracks by Ryoji Ikeda that Richard presents in Chapter 4 set up, for me, an interesting dichotomy. On the one hand, there is a mechanized conception of time—what Richard describes as an "abstracted exploration into the sculpting and processing of individual sonic pulses"—strictly iterative and highly periodic, and on the other there is our own subjective experience of time—how we make sense of such persistent regularity. Jennie and I spent a great deal of time discussing these aspects. She spoke to me of the strong physical effect of the music upon her, its relentless and insistent qualities, and the difficulty in preserving her "own subjectivity." I found the listening experience less of an affront upon my psyche but similarly struggled to process what I was listening to due to the incessant nature of the music and the lack of immediate contrast across the three tracks.

As Richard tells us early in the chapter, the types of beat patterns presented are those most generally associated with electronic dance music. Here, though, Ikeda takes a more radical approach by stripping back the music to only its most essential qualities—those of pulsation and timbral manipulation. I heard distinctions in sound coming principally from timbral manipulations of these pulses, which occurred either gradually or as sudden spectral shifts. My focus was on observing the beating patterns, through which the nuances of these spectral sweeps could be observed. The three tracks are somewhat similar in presentation and, as such, gave me the impression of lab tones subjected to slightly different treatments.

Upon closer listening, however, I became aware of some clear differences in these tracks. It is not necessary to discuss the particularities of each track here as Richard outlines distinctions between each in his chapter.

However, some observations of what I identified may clarify certain points made elsewhere in this postlude. The first track (track 4) opens with quiet pulsations and an identifiable high pitch, almost outside of audible range. The sonic sweeps across the frequency range are subtle, but transformative and there is a distinct sense of the music getting louder as it continues. It is difficult to tell whether this perceived increase in amplitude is due to lower frequencies becoming foregrounded over time, or due to an actual increase in volume. This gradual build cuts off abruptly at 2:51. The second track (track 5) seemed to outline greater degrees of sonic manipulation than the first. I observed the pulses as being more clearly defined while accentuations created for me a sense of temporal dislocation and the illusion of inherent rhythms. At just over five minutes, this track is somewhat longer than the first. The cutoff appeared equally as abruptly. The third track (track 6), which is almost eleven minutes, is by far the longest, containing more varied spectral transitions. As with the second, I observed that it was more heavily reliant on lower-range frequencies.

Richard speaks of "auditory hallucinations" that he experiences and of the persistent temptation to search for rhythmic patterns within the pulse. Eric F. Clarke in his book, *Ways of Listening*, says:

> Perception is a self-tuning process, in which the pick-up of environmental information is intrinsically reinforcing, so that the system self-adjusts so as to optimize its resonance with the environment .... Perception is essentially exploratory, seeking out sources of stimulation in order to discover more about the environment.[1]

Correspondingly, I find myself scanning and searching the auditory surface of the work as I listen to each track. In track 5 in particular, I find myself focusing most specifically upon the timbral shifts, whereas in the previous track it was upon the regularity of the pulse. The act of searching for meaning makes my listening active and more rewarding, but this is no easy search. I may observe certain frequency shifts that change the character of the pulse but this is always pitted against the machine-like insistence of the pulse. The experience, for me, is not unlike listening to the work of certain noise artists. As with the work of Merzbow or Dror Feiler, I have to mentally prepare myself for being and staying in that place. Jennie has also spoken of the difficulty of sustained listening to the Ikeda tracks over time.

I was intrigued by Richard's observation that the speed of the pulses presented here is not directly related to temporal flow rate. I also found that the ongoing pulsation removes any direct sense of teleology. It is perhaps this that can account for the varying lengths of the tracks that utilize similar material. As Richard noted, our sense of moving forward comes more directly from the changes in timbre over time. The sweeping motion carries with it a shape, a trajectory that can be navigated. Perhaps one of the intriguing aspects of these pieces is their ability to present sound that is both arrested and in motion. The pulses are of such speed and regularity that they almost become immobile, while the timbral aspect is active and subject to change. If we can speak of segmentation at all in these tracks, this occurs most in those moments where the spectral sweep quickly changes (such as in track 5), offering us a clear point of delineation within the processing of events. Richard speaks of anticipating the effects of these timbral sweeps. I listened again with this in mind and found myself following their trajectory. There appears to be something performative about these sweeps, as if the oscillation is being controlled by a human in real time, taking us somewhere.

In Richard's chapter, he speaks of the difficulty of recall in this music; Jennie and I also discussed the problems of remembering these tracks. The beginning of the next track almost seems to obliterate any memory of the previous one. As I listen to track 5, I try to recall the speed of track 4. Was it the same as that of the one I am listening to? I struggle to tell. The sheer speed and directness of the music hammers home a sense of its presence, making notions of the past largely redundant. If I am to make sense of this experience, I must submit to its incessant nature and then listen and follow. To recollect is perhaps to miss the point.

Ikeda presents us with music that is overwhelming despite its minimal means of construction. It operates at a speed that is beyond our immediate perception and sustains itself over time through sculpting and shaping the constant outpouring of simple, iterative pulses. There is perhaps something akin to operating machinery in this piece; one must keep the machine switched on and let it run for it to do its job effectively, while at the same time keeping a constant eye on its manner of operation, occasionally nudging it this way or that to keep it on course. If I am to keep on track with this music, I must follow its navigation and observe, rather than make sense of, its temporal flow.

Note

1   Eric F. Clarke, *Ways of Listening: An Ecological Approach to the Perception of Musical Meaning* (Oxford: Oxford University Press, 2012), 19.

CHAPTER FIVE

Granulated Time: Toshiya Tsunoda's *O Kokos Tis Anixis*

Jennie Gottschalk

Toshiya Tsunoda is a Japanese sound artist who works primarily with field recordings. *O Kokos Tis Anixis* (Grains of Spring)[1] (2013) is unusual among his works in its manipulation of the temporalities of the recordings. He more frequently changes the listening perspective through the ingenious configurations of microphones. This work is distinctly related to his larger body of work, though, in that it places the listener in a situation which calls forth a subjective response. In his substantial article on Tsunoda's work, Michael Pisaro writes:

> Observation is Toshiya Tsunoda's word for listening, and that shade of difference between the two words (observation/listening) is important. Observation carries an echo of object and objectivity. It places itself between object and subject, in a continuum where the fog of our senses operates.
>
> Tsunoda's work over the past 20 years explores the complexity of this continuum in a dense variety of radical and often quite beautiful ways.[2]

This chapter is a consideration of my own observation of this one piece as it affects my sense of temporality and subjectivity, which become inextricably linked in this context.

The workings of *O Kokos Tis Anixis* can—like the plots of many great literary works—be very briefly explained: Field recordings of the Miura

Peninsula in Japan are the foundational content of eight tracks over the length of two CDs. There are about sixty loops inserted that are made of the material of the recordings. This brief summary does not begin to convey the particularities of the work and their impact on my sense of temporal stasis and flow. The loops contain nothing new other than their temporal framing, but they have a completely different impact from their source material.

Subjective retellings of each track

Though I had spent some time with this work in the past, it took me some time to begin to find my way through it again. I found that I needed to have a clear sense of the basic behaviors of the tracks on their own terms before I could find a workable approach to the piece as a whole. Each track is distinctive in duration, type of location, time of day, and the nature of the looping treatment. I found that I had trouble remembering the details of these behaviors, so I made a set of charts to reference and refine over successive listenings, each of which is included below before the track's prose description. Inevitably, these descriptions also become quite subjective. My response to the final track is by far the most extensive, since this is the section that was, for me, the most perceptually complex.

The loops will be discussed on their own terms later, but I'll discuss their temporal impacts in context in this first survey of the piece. Even without this looping treatment, the raw field recordings have temporal implications in the frequency and intensity of audible activity—whether it be animal or human, natural or mechanical.

The sounds of small fruits falling in the grass as the wind shook the tree

The first track reveals a bright daytime scene filled with bird sounds. Almost immediately, there is a rapid looping of a very small sample drawn from that moment in the recording, followed by an abrupt return to the direct, untouched recording, as if nothing had happened. Another loop follows closely afterward which is slightly more complex, with more audible components to the sample, and lasts a little longer (twelve seconds rather than six). The third, 43-second loop has a greater sense of weight. It is quickly clear that the loops are each handcrafted. Beyond having different numbers of iterations, sample durations, and corresponding total durations, they are each made out of their own characteristic source material that has been carefully selected and treated. These three loops have highly distinctive behaviors and characteristics. The fourth loop, around the four-minute mark, has a percussive quality, like a kind of boring in or drilling.

Table 5.1 the sounds of small fruits falling in the grass as the wind shook the tree (17:46)

Loop #	Start time	End time	# seconds	# iterations	Effect (subjective)
1	0:17	0:23	6	101*	not much dimension
2	1:01	1:13	12	100	primarily one noise, but background comes through when slowed
3	2:01	2:44	43	101	not much dimension
4	3:50	4:04	14	101	drilling
5	4:20	7:11	171	100	extended moment, circles between distinct events
6	7:12	7:17	5	101	something between drilling and buzzing
7	7:18	7:18	1	—	sounds like a single tone
8	7:32	7:34	2	—	sounds like a single tone
9	8:40	9:30	50	32	adds another dimension to the landscape
10	11:13	11:23	10	101	hammering
11	15:40	16:23	43	30	muted cuckoo clock
12	16:28	17:13	45	101	dig

* Tsunoda writes in the notes to the release that "parts are repeated between three and a hundred times." I'm not sure whether I counted these wrong or that was an approximation, but for consistency I'll chart what I heard when I slowed the recordings down.

Around 4:20, the loop feels circular in shape, not just in name, perhaps because the elements of the original sample are so distinct that I get the mental image of traveling between them. It lasts for quite some time, almost three minutes, becoming its own extended moment. Introducing this piece, Tsunoda writes:

> The ancient Greek philosophers thought that the world is constituted of a series of grains of space and time. When I walked around Miura Peninsula in the springtime, I felt the same way—the quality of the space and the time seemed to be formed by a series of grains of sounds.[3]

This moment in the first track offers me a firsthand experience of that observation. In selecting this succession of sounds to loop, Tsunoda has pointed to an example of this alignment between the grains of time and the grains of space. The isolation of this moment from the sounds immediately preceding and following it delineates a grain out of what would otherwise be an unbroken flow. While I can only imagine the grains of that space, the grains of that time are presented and then traced through repetition, which affords me a duration to observe this moment closely.

Several other brief loops follow, each of which is very distinct. I have the feeling that I'm not living in the original landscape that was recorded, but in the varied succession of shapes, durations, and characters of the loops. Approaching the nine-minute mark is a looping of birdsong, evoking a mechanized bird in its repetition. Birdsong itself is often repetitive, and the repetitions following the loop are perhaps untreated, but their appearance following this particular loop invites comparison to the looping of birdsong by Tsunoda. I am reminded that repetition occurs in nature, as well as through technological interventions. A purely synthetic sounding loop interrupts the flow, and then another sounds quite persistent and percussive. The pace relaxes, and time passes without interruption for several minutes starting at 12:00. Then at 15:42, all that comes to a grinding halt with an extended loop that includes four sounds. I start to hear it as a muted cuckoo clock, with the regular chirping and percussive sounds. A different loop follows immediately afterward that seems to dig into the ground, becoming further entrenched with each iteration. For half a minute there is more of the field recording, as if to briefly remind me of the setting that all of this activity was drawn from.

The sequence of the chirp sounds of a bush warbler

Track 2 is much shorter at 6:10, and again seems clearly to be placed in daytime hours. Drops of water and the song of a bush warbler predominate.

Table 5.2 the sequence of the chirp sounds of a bush warbler (6:10)

Loop #	Start time	End time	# seconds	# iterations	Effect (subjective)
1	1:31	1:37	6	101	hammering
2	1:48	1:54	6	5	sharp
3	2:14	2:15	1	30	pecking
4	2:16	2:16	1	—	pecking
5	2:17	2:18	1	30	pecking
6	2:18	2:18	1	30	abrupt, high pitched
7	2:51	2:56	4	100	hammering/pecking
8	2:57	3:04	7	101	hammering/pecking
9	4:41	5:12	31	30	pecking

The song itself is looped, first unrecognizably—because of the extreme brevity of the sample—and then in a more identifiable loop. Four brief, distinct loops of small samples follow, and then release back into the original recording. Two rapid loops around the three-minute mark are evidently of birdsong, but they quicken the pace considerably. Following that, the bird performs its own repetitions. Around 4:42, one high sample is repeated with a clear articulation (with a distinct break in sound between each iteration), giving a metronomic sense of pulse. Time is relaxed in the raw recording, and loops are anticipated as a heightening of tension. The outside sounds feel more familiar than the ever-changing loops, offering a kind of rest or haven from these interventions.

The various events happening in the temple precincts in the mountain

Track 3 has one unobtrusive loop around the two-minute mark, but it maintains a relaxed atmosphere and doesn't even seem to be a loop without attentive listening. (I missed it in several early listenings. That may have something to do with its slow rate of repetition.) As the "various events" take place all around the audible area, the prevalent question for me in this track is not when, but where. Where are each of these sounds taking place, and what are the spatial relationships between them? The loops appear aperiodically. Unlike the previous tracks, in this case I am not waiting for a loop. But then one occurs, very briefly, at 7:30, as if to remind me that the recorded material is still subject to this treatment, even if it is only exercised sparsely. The looping does not break the flow of the interchange of sounds throughout the space. Finally, leading up to 18:00 there is an obvious loop, involving many different types of sounds throughout the space. Because the sounds seem to be pulled from sources all over the location, they collectively imply a sense of breadth. Similarly to the "grains of space and time" mentioned in reference to the first track, the (audible) qualities of the space—in this case its expansiveness—align with an expansive and relaxed sense of temporality. There are a few more sounds, including birdsong, sirens, and the voices of children, and then the track ends.

Table 5.3 the various events happening in the temple precincts in the mountain (20:47)

Loop #	Start time	End time	# seconds	# iterations	Effect (subjective)
1	1:58	2:18	20	7	clapping
2	7:32	7:32	1	6	percussive
3	17:56	19:20	84	30	vastness

The echoed sounds in a vacant lot as the night fell gradually

Track 4 has one loop near the start that seems to include many different sound sources, and repeats a number of times, each repetition lasting just over one second. It hovers on the edge of breaking the flow without ever fully doing so. Perhaps what I hear as the distance between sound sources within the loop—the broad range of space it seems to cover—makes it seem like it is traveling through space as well as time for these thirty-eight seconds, rather than being a point of stoppage or stasis. A moment of birdsong is captured and frozen just after the six-minute mark, but it seems to spin out and sustain that sound, rather than breaking a sense of flow.

The significant trajectory in this track is not from looping to uninterrupted, but, as its name implies, from light to dark. The timescale and the basic nature of that transition feels familiar from everyday life—the regular 24- hour cycle that has experienced transitions from day to night and back. The track does not juxtapose direct and looped recordings. The synthetic sounding loops are brief, and the more naturalistic ones are sometimes longer. The third loop is extremely brief, and the fourth is quiet, unobtrusive, and only lasts for ten seconds. There is a careful balance so that the loops are either too short or too slight, a departure to interrupt the overall flow of time passing.

The sounds of three branches falling down on a tin roof of a small roadside shrine

The daytime scene is interrupted by a fast, synthetic sounding loop before the first minute is finished. Another loop is unobtrusive two minutes later, but the sounds of birds and of the wind are most prevalent until a quick succession of rapid loops. None of them last for more than a moment,

Table 5.4 the echoed sounds in a vacant lot as the night fell gradually (27:59)

Loop #	Start time	End time	# seconds	# iterations	Effect (subjective)
1	1:40	2:18	38	31	as if the echoing itself is being caught, expands the field
2	6:04	6:06	2	31	like an accent
3	15:37	15:38	1	8	small rupture
4	17:53	18:03	10	12	mechanical

Table 5.5 the sounds of three branches falling down on a tin roof of a small roadside shrine (9:20)

Loop #	Start time	End time	# seconds	# iterations	Effect (subjective)
1	0:46	0:48	2	51	abrupt drilling
2	3:00	3:24	24	8	gentle
3	5:21	5:24	3	51	tension/restfulness
4	5:25	5:39	14	51	digs a small hole
5	5:39	5:41	2	—	digs a tiny hole
6	8:04	8:12	8	50	woodpecker type insistence

Table 5.6 the high-pitched sounds that occurred momentarily when the tree branches rustled as the wind shook the tree (11:31)

Loop #	Start time	End time	# seconds	# iterations	Effect (subjective)
1	3:53	3:54	1	6	drills a hole
2	3:54	3:55	1	6	drills a hole
3	4:11	4:15	4	11	carves a small hole
4	4:45	4:52	7	12	sharp
5	5:20	5:20	1	6	prick
6	6:55	7:03	8	11	prick
7	10:28	10:31	3	11	prick

but the succession creates a clear breakage in the track. These sounds are probably the tree branches mentioned in the title. The overall track offers the setting, and these isolated moments are events that take place within that setting.

The high-pitched sounds that occurred momentarily when the tree branches rustled as the wind shook the tree

Track 6 presents a setting of insects, children, birds, and wind. Loops begin to appear after several minutes. They are all brief, but each has a distinct pitch and pace. The time between them gradually becomes less frequent, but what began as a settled-in feeling becomes an anticipation of when the next loop might take place and how it will operate. Events such as the flowing of a small stream of water eventually overtake this anticipation, and are only briefly interrupted once more.

The sounds happening in a pond and its surroundings

Track 7 has a brief loop near the start that suspends my sense of the flow of time to some degree. A longer fragment is repeated two minutes later. It is only because of the difference between the repeated elements that I can clearly tell that it is a loop. A percussive sound is juxtaposed with two pitches from a bird. For about ten minutes following that I hear no loops at all, other than the birds' own repetitions within their songs. I get to know the different types of sound and listen for how they interlock. Then there is a sudden percussive interruption (not a loop), but it perforates rather than breaks the flow. The repetitions performed by the birds themselves at around 17:30 are compelling, and present a kind of sonic foreground. My sense of what is looped and what is regular birdsong gets tested around 19:00. I'm not sure which is which, and I have become accustomed to the presence of both. Then at 22:13 there is a triangulation between three very different sounds: birdsong, a drop, and air noise. These are some of the various sounds referenced in the title.

The sounds of ashes burning in the fire built by fishermen

From the opening of the track, there is a constant flow of activity: numerous bird calls at various distances, insect noises, sweeping, human speech, footsteps, and the sounds of the fire. There are so many components of this sound world, and I'm constantly switching my attention between them, zooming in on close sounds and out on more distant ones. The listening angle is simultaneously wide and narrow. How does that affect temporal perception? Generally speaking, the wider angle has fewer boundaries and a more fluid presentation. The closer sounds, whether or not they are looped, present urgency and pulse. They put me *in time*, and also make me more aware of the moments that allow me to remove myself from it.

Table 5.7 the sounds happening in a pond and its surroundings (23:43)

Loop #	Start time	End time	# seconds	# iterations	Effect (subjective)
1	1:20	1:37	17	50	enveloping, suspenseful
2	3:24	4:22	58	7	loose and long
3	19:04	19:07	3	17	hammering
4	22:13	22:36	23	11	open, multiple locations

Table 5.8 the sounds of ashes bursting in the fire built by fishermen (29:16)

Loop #	Start time	End time	# seconds	# iterations	Effect (subjective)
1	1:54	2:51	57	50	total stoppage, appears to be skipping
2	3:40	3:59	19	15	diminutive clicking
3	5:02	5:30	28	10	sweeping sound
4	6:35	7:26	51	16	cumbersome
5	20:22	20:53	31	31	shoveling into the ground
6	22:04	23:18	74	50	I feel absolutely stuck the moment before being released.
7	24:10	24:33.	23	101	harsh stoppage
8	28:41	29:11.	30	30	light thud

The sounds of the ashes initially appear aperiodically and inconspicuously. At 1:54, there is one barely noticeable ash sound, and then it is looped fifty times over, each iteration lasting just over a second. It is percussive and grainy, and though the sample never changes, I hear different things in it as it continues. It completely stops the flow, lasting almost a minute, and brings me out of the music and out of the space. I have moved from imaginary inhabiting to a more analytical mode. It is a digital intervention. The sample has become a tiny repeated tile. It is obviously the same every time, but I hear different dimensions and qualities in it as it moves forward. At first I remark on the rhythmic and percussive quality of its iteration, then notice a slight downward tendency in its pitch profile and the harmonics that seem to be present. I become aware of my own removal from the setting and the opportunity to hear the actual sound of the ashes more directly. Finally, a little over halfway through, I am impatient to get back to that setting. My sense of place has been derailed, and I want it back. My aural impression of this setting is one of warmth, quiet action, and fresh sea air. But the loop, lasting half the time of all of that preceding material, has obscured everything that came before it. Then all of a sudden I am back in the direct recording, as if nothing had happened.

This moment makes me aware of the line that tends to be drawn between an analytical mode and a more relaxed mode—processing something versus settling into it. Field recording often brings up these issues, since it can evoke the experience of inhabiting space. Why do I hear the switch from a more diverse range of sounds to a static repetition as disruptive? It could simply be that I enjoy the one more than the other. But the two modes are also equivalent to moving (people moving, hearing different sounds around me) and stopping. The flow of events is literally stopped in time—disrupted. But it presents an opportunity to learn what to listen for over the course of the thirty-minute track. True to the title, all of the loops are of ashes bursting. Once the recording resumes, it takes just a moment and then all of the initial flurry of activity is resumed.

Various strands of that activity over the next minute are carried into the second loop that begins at 3:40. While the first loop was focused minutely on what sounds like a single burst of ash, the second includes what sounds like a buzzing insect, distant birdsong, and a set of three ash sounds. It only lasts nineteen seconds, a third of the time of the previous loop, and the sample duration is slightly longer. It makes a very different impression, placing me in a triangulation of sounds, rather than a comparatively simple iteration. Perceptually it doesn't cause the same kind of interruption, both because it is shorter and because it suggests a variation on the flow of attention between different sound sources. I didn't notice until many listenings in that it seems to be slightly slowed down from the raw recording. (This slowing of the looped material may occur elsewhere as well, but I have not specifically found it.) The pitch of the passing insect sounds a minor third lower in the loop than otherwise. But despite that, the departure from the loop feels like a slowing down, a relaxing, a settling in.

Just after the five-minute mark, another loop picks up that is more open than the previous one. If the first loop felt like an insistent percussive sound (a point), the second feels like a looser triangulation, and the third is more of a rounded square. The squareness of it is the *four*-ness of it, a sequence of sounds that seems to ask to be counted as four pulses, and the rounding is accomplished by the quality of the sounds. Again there is bursting ash, but it is a longer clip than before, and the sweeping sound that is also present has a distinctly rounded quality to me. The result of this more open space is that I don't feel a stoppage at all, and for the moment my sense of time, parallel to my sense of the space, does not contain any delineation. If anything, what I feel is a restful acceleration. The fourth loop continues at a similar pace to the third, also with an easily counted pulse of four, but feels less rounded, being comprised mostly of more percussive ash sounds.

Following these first four loops, there is a long stretch of recording in which nothing is looped. There is a significant opportunity to settle into the flow of events. At 9:15, I begin to hear a sound, either a plane or a long gust of wind that becomes more and more present over the course of more than a minute. It expands the dimensions of the time interval, creating a larger unit that is nothing like a pulse but a perfectly rounded increase and decrease of amplitude. This motion expands the sense of audible space in both height and distance, and correspondingly expands the perceived temporal scale. The birds are still making themselves heard, and enforce this sense of a inhabiting a broader space. The same thing happens again in a more prolonged way after the twelve-minute mark, and then once more after the fifteen-minute mark. Bird calls repeat and create natural loops. The level of activity seems to be gradually changing. I can't tell if that is because there are no more planes passing, or because there haven't been loops for so long.

Just before 14:00, the appearance of birds signals a change in light or time of day. The pulses of seagull tones give an occasional rhythmic grounding around 14:50, and footsteps (from what I can tell) lend a loose periodicity to the sound over these two minutes. There is a continuing increase of sounding bird activity, and the bird sounds create natural loops. People are talking. Then at 20:22 there is a succession of thirty-one ash bursts. Despite this abrupt switch, I find it hard to switch back into a looping mode, and repeatedly find myself trying to explain its intense rhythmic quality as an original occurrence, rather than being Tsunoda's decision after the recording was made. The percussive ash bursts are followed by a succession of quieter, less prominent sounds.

The sixth loop, unlike any before or after it in this track, includes a total cessation of sound that is more of a removal from the sound world than anything that precedes it. The sample duration is only about 1.5 seconds, but each of its fifty iterations[4] feels like a break from the space and a total removal from any sense of flow or presence. All the variations in loop duration, shape, and various other qualities have, taken together, offered a small amount of preparation toward this moment, but an insufficient one. It is an ejection. It anticipates the end of the track, though that is still six minutes off.

When this succession of removals suddenly ends, there is more audible activity than ever, including various bird, human, water, and ash sounds. Another plane passes by. The next sound that is sampled is the shortest by far, lasting only a quarter of a second. It creates an urgency and intensification. Like the opening loop it is definitely a point, and an abrupt, hammering one at that, rather than a fuller shape. After a few more minutes of uninterrupted activity (more footsteps, fewer sounds of ashes), there is a series of light thuds—a very short, truncated sound occurring about once a second that is looped thirty times. Six seconds after it ends, the track is over. It is a gentle but decisive exit from this highly detailed sound world.

It seems to me that this track has a different behavior from the others. While the first track introduces many of the mechanisms of the work, and others explore a number of different settings and looping decisions, in this one I can use all that prior listening experience toward temporal type of listening that is simultaneously more open and more focused. I feel as if I've been taught in the first seven tracks how the loops can behave—the various sample lengths, numbers of iterations, the wide range of source material, degree of contrast within a sample, total duration, degree of interference, density or sparsity of placement within the track, and so on. In the final track, the growing shapes of the loops and their several different timescales gradually expand into the center of the track, in which the original recording is presented without interference. The departure from these timescales is a sort of removal from the scene on multiple levels: through abruptness (loop five), removal of sound (loop six), hammer-like insistence (loop seven), and, finally, a light, anticlimactic thud.

Gérard Grisey spoke of bird time, human time, and whale time.[5] In this track, there is bird time, ash time, human (footstep/speech) time, and airflow time. We travel among these levels, but it is the ash time that becomes the object of focus. That is the component of the sound that would most likely be missed, or just barely noticed, without Tsunoda's naming and intervention. The fishermen built the fire, but in its detailed occurrence it is never within their control. The minute treatment of these ash sounds through looping brings that irregularity into focus. The sounds start out bare, unornamented, and return to that state. I could have missed these short, dry sounds if it were not for the careful treatment of this and all the other tracks, and the learning process that emerged from careful listening.

Spatial and temporal perception

Two things gradually became clear to me as I spent time with this piece. The first one is about the piece itself: Each of the tracks has its own means of engaging with time. Aside from the obvious differences in settings and durations of the tracks, they are also differentiated through the duration, frequency, and degree of invasiveness of the loops within them.

The second thing that became clear from these listenings may be my own peculiarity. I learned that I often think of time in spatial terms. I recalled when I first learned about a timeline, when the oldest dates were on the left and we traveled closer to the present as we went further to the right. In my current work doing audio transcription, I put the sound file at the top of the screen in Quicktime and watch the time marker gradually move from left to right. But those are two-dimensional examples. *O Kokos Tis Anixis* activates my conception of time in relation to my imagination of a three-dimensional space. Various locations, times of day, and natural or manmade features are mentioned in the titles of each piece. That information, combined with the material I hear, give me a sense of the spatial scope (radius, perhaps) of each recording, which also suggests a temporal scope. A plane flying overhead signals a broader scope, both in its height and for the fact that it travels in and out of the recorded frame. That has a relaxing effect. When I can hear that progress, I am sure that no looping is occurring.

Within the loops, those that have a single source seem to operate on a smaller scale, both temporally and spatially. I often referred to them in my notes with terms like "pricking," "hammering," "drilling," and "digging in." A sonic microscope is placed on a single action in a single place, and through repetition it assumes a guise of industriousness. With that sense of industriousness often comes some feeling of stress, and in those moments loops seem to take on a hurried sort of tension.

Conversely, the loops that occur over what I imagine to be a broader physical range (e.g., track 3 loop 2, track 4 loop 1, and track 7 loops 2 and 4) give a sense of being back out in the open air that is far more like the untouched stretches of the field recordings than the more focused loops. They also give me an equivalent sense of rest, or freedom from constraint. The repetitions are revealing, rather than masking, the diversity of activities and sonic points of interest in the audible area. They do not hammer in, but project out, both spatially and temporally. My sense of time passing is narrow or broad, corresponding to my sense of the space that is being traversed from one moment, section, or piece to another. That narrowness/broadness spectrum does not correspond directly to a sense of a shorter or longer duration, but instead to degrees of restfulness or intensity. Extreme examples in either direction are most likely to distort my sense of how much time has passed, but the direction of that shift (less time or more time) is unpredictable from one instance to another.

Profiles of the loops in content and impact

While the field recordings are compelling as raw material, it is the looping that steers my listening throughout, particularly in my experience of temporal flow. Certain aspects of the looping are helpful to describe in building up an understanding of how the work operates.

Loop quantity and placement within each track

With a total duration of 17:46, the first track has twelve loops fairly evenly spaced throughout. This section announces the technique that is being used, and presents it consistently and with enough variations that the sample content, sample duration, number of iterations, and total duration can be understood as a complex set of variables. The second track is more brief, but also has fairly consistent loops, though they are far more weighted toward the beginning of the track in rapid succession. The third track, which is on the longer side, only has two loops near the beginning and another toward the end. The fourth track has a similar profile, with the one difference being that there are two very short loops that interrupt the fifteen minutes between the longer ones. The fifth track is rather short, at 9:20, and two longer loops dominate the middle third. There is one brief loop after each of these longer ones, and one eight-second loop that takes place about a minute before the close. There is a fairly fast succession of five loops in track 6, starting just before the four-minute mark and ending at 5:20. Two more brief loops appear sporadically during the remaining six minutes. In the nearly twenty-four minutes of track 7, two loops appear within the first five minutes and two within the last five minutes. I could not hear any loops between 4:22 and 19:04. In the final track, the loops are again more heavily weighted toward the opening and close, but this time there are four on each end, with an uninterrupted flow of field recording of nearly thirteen minutes.

What do these different profiles reveal? The loops pick up on certain types of sounds, usually those named in the title of the track. These sounds are discovered through patience, and appear without regularity. As Tsunoda writes, "The only way for us to relate to the events is to closely observe what is happening there."[6] The sounds that are named and sought after in each track may not appear for some time.

Another way of thinking about it is that the frequency of loops in the early tracks is a cue for future listening, and their appearances then become more of a variable. Stretches that span over ten minutes without any looping allow for a greater focus on the flow of sounds in the environment. Anticipation of interference eventually gives way to direct attention to the unfolding of events in time and place. This attention takes on greater focus because of the looping treatment of the samples prior to it.

Longest and shortest loops in total duration

The loop with the longest total duration (nearly three minutes) begins at 4:20 in the first track. It seems to sweep through much of the audible space in a wide, fairly rapid (but still trackable) circle. The buzzing of an insect, two sounds of objects dropping (likely the fruit named in the title), and wind noise cycle through a hundred times, last just under two seconds each time. The repetition is exact, as it is in every loop, but it never feels static. The motion is simply caught between this limited set of sounds. There is an opportunity to hear them in relation to each other, drawing the imagined audible space closer together. In my early notes on the piece, I described this moment as "churning through, a push and a click, a push and a click. It sounds like gentle machinery."[7] A month later I wrote, "Long loops feel like films. Something is happening repeatedly and it becomes visual and visceral."[8]

The second longest loop is near the end of the final track, at 22:04. "I feel absolutely stuck the moment before being released," I wrote.[9] I referred to it later as a total stoppage: "Flow is utterly broken with all the iterations." It also sounded to me like the CD was skipping, as "one sound with aftersounds."[10] Where the loop described in the previous paragraph feels like it is moving between sounding elements, this one feels stuck, likely because it is dominated by a single sound source. Because there is no sense of travel through the recorded space, there is also no sense of moving through time. This is stasis, stoppage. The same is true of the first loop in that same final track.

The other long loops are more like the first one, in that the numerous elements within each sample present me with a sense of motion which is both visual (spatial) and aural (temporal) and has the broader effect of avoiding a sense of stasis over the course of the repetition. The third and final loop in the third track captures many events within the three seconds or so of the sample. The three percussive sounds in the loop sound like some type of machinery, but they are offset by two birds that are also audible. The louder bird seems to precipitate the percussive sounds, and the other bird seems to comment on the series of events. If this sequence were not repeated, I would have no real opportunity for such a speculation. While I know it is impossible, during this repeated, wide-ranging loop my mind's eye pictures one bird slightly suspended, driving some type of machinery with a fierce call, while another somewhere above comments on the proceedings. The first loop in track 4 also has percussive elements, but they are part of a more evidently vast landscape, including what seems to me to be an echo (as mentioned in the title) and the chattering of birds. Though the sample is just over a second long, I have the sense of scanning a large area, not all of which would be visible from a single position. While it's not an aerial view in perspective, it similarly offers a wider perception of the field. This panning out is not a removal from the flow of this field recording, but a more thorough immersion in it. Though the details of the second loop of track 7 are different, it has a very similar effect on me for the same reasons of implying a larger field and a diversity of activity. The final loop of track 7 is more like the loop first described in this paragraph, in that its two types of sound imply vertical space but not an expanse. It travels up and down, rather than around, and feels more like a pulse than a swoop.

While some of the loops with short durations appear as singular interruptions, others are grouped together in close succession. This occurs after the four-minute mark in track 1. After a loop that lasts for nearly three minutes, the next one lasts for five seconds, and the third for about one second. This track, and this section of the track in particular, seems to be designed to reveal the behavior of the piece of looping at different rates for different durations. A similar presentation occurs after the five-minute mark in track 5. Track 2 has a notable sequence of four very short loops, each lasting a second or less. Each loop has a distinctive pitch, and taken together they make up what sounds like both a sequence and a melody. In pursuing this line of thought, it occurs to me to look back at the title of the track, "the sequence of the chirp sounds of a bush warbler." This sequence of loops is a clear presentation of the focus of the piece.

Number of iterations of each sample

Another variable with these loops is how many times they are iterated. I was surprised to find that most of the loops in track 1 occur about a hundred times. Several of the loops in track 2 have this many iterations, but it doesn't happen again until the second to last loop in the final track. The perceptual effect of this number of iterations feels related to the sense of eventfulness in each piece. Tracks 1 and 2 both have a fairly consistent rate of presentation of the loops. The total lengths of these loops vary widely, and they are either long in total duration or dense with activity. Other numbers of iterations that are common throughout the set hover around six, eleven, thirty, and fifty.

Track 6 has the fewest number of iterations overall, ranging from six to twelve. The loops start nearly four minutes into the track, and five of them follow in rather close succession. Because of their brevity (never more than eight seconds, usually four or less), and also because of the variety of pitches and textures within each brief loop, they seem to be very much part of the flow of sound events. They highlight the passing sounds, rather than creating their own environments. These limited repetitions make me more aware of and more present with the details of this setting, rather than ever feeling like a removal from that setting.

Visceral effects of the loops

A few images kept recurring as my impressions of the loops. Some of them had a hammering quality. Others were more focused, often higher pitched, and seemed more like a pricking or piercing than a hammering. Another set of loops felt more like a dig. Each iteration seemed to enforce the ones before it, taking on more gravity or weight. A couple of these were long in their total duration (including track 8, loop 5, which I described as "shoveling into the ground"[11]), but others were very short (as in track 6: "drills a hole," "carves a small hole"). The looping alters my sense of the dimensions of the space. Just a few of the loops, all within either the first or the last track (1–11, 8–1, 8–6, 8–7) felt like a total stoppage. They were all rather long in total duration, though the samples were not always long. Others such as 4–3 were much shorter, only lasting about a second, but created a small rupture in the flow of the track.

* * *

Spending a significant amount of time with this work has caused me to ask myself questions that had never occurred to me before, and I have become aware of a correlation in my thinking between an imagined space and a perceived temporality. Does time pass differently in a triangle than it does in a circle or a trapezoid, a vertical line or a diagonal line? When there are clearly defined points in the sound and those points are drawn into a loop, they operate as a pulse, or at least as one part of a repeating series. The most dominant sound is liable to be perceived as the ictus. If there are several dominant sounds, they become several pulses, as in the triangles of 7–2, 7–4, and 8–2, or the trapezoid of 3–3. These shapes have points and edges. They might feel big, but they are defined. I learn to follow them, to count along.

On the other hand, when the sounds do not have as clear of a definition, or some of them seem to travel, they feel like circles, such as 1–5 and the sweeping sound of 8–3. In these instances, I no longer count the time passing. A moment becomes extended, or sweeps through. I am outside of time's passage, rather than called into it, whereas the presence of clear points or pulses puts me back into a type of clock time, however modified it might be. The same clock time is equally, or sometimes even more, provoked by samples that travel back and forth between two distinct sounds. The up and down, back and forth, is like a pendulum, and I am caught in it in both directions.

The impact of this piece, for me, is in the vast difference in the effects of the various loops. Some loops interrupt the flow. Others seem to extend and envelop the space. Other loops make the events within the recording more apparent. Some of the loops make me sit up and take notice, while some cause me to lose time completely. All of these decisions are made— so very effectively—with an otherwise unprocessed recording of everyday occurrences. Though the overall setting of the Japanese Miura Peninsula is quite different from my own in suburban New England, it gives me the sense that I can choose how to mark my own everyday time. It can be pulsed or unpulsed, observed minutely or as a vast flow. My agency in that perception has been opened up through close listening to this work.

Notes

1   Toshiya Tsunoda, *O Kokos Tis Anixis* (Grains of Spring), edition.t, e.04, 2013, 2 compact discs.

2   Michael Pisaro, "Membrane—Window—Mirror: (The folded worlds of Toshiya Tsunoda)," *Surround* 3 (2015), http://surround.noquam.com/membrane-window-mirror.

3   Tsunoda writes in the notes to the release that "parts are repeated between three and a hundred times." I'm not sure whether I counted these wrong or that was an approximation, but for consistency I'll chart what I heard when I slowed the recordings down.

4   I counted these iterations while playing back the recording at one-tenth of the original speed.

5   See http://brahms.ircam.fr/works/work/8977.

6   Tsunoda, *Grains of Spring*. Back cover.

7   Author notes, January 13, 2017.

8   Author notes, February 10, 2017.

9   Author notes, February 9, 2017.

10   Author notes, February 13, 2017.

11   Author notes, March 30, 2017.

Postlude to Chapter Five

Bryn Harrison

It might be said that there are two types of presence in the world: on the one hand, there is the presence of what we experience directly—a reality that is both physical and tangible; and on the other, there is presence of memory—distorted but somehow no less real. Sometimes, as I go about my daily life, I find myself alive to the world around me, perceptive and responsive to what I see, hear, and feel, while at other times I get so lost in thought that the world seems shut off, transporting me to another place. These two types of presence seem somehow inseparable; the transitions between what I experience and what I remember experiencing are rarely severe; the immediate present also has a hint of the past and the future ("the meeting ground for memory and anticipation," as Jonathan Kramer put it[1]) and past memories are similarly prompted by lived experiences. In fact, the ways in which my perception shifts between experience and memory is so seamless that I am usually unaware of a shift between them.

There are times, however, when the cut between the past and the present is severe; an alarm goes off, jolting me back to the "now," or the sudden experience of déjà vu, transporting me immediately to the past. The contrast between the gradual unfolding of time and the retrieval of the immediate past in Tsunoda's *O Kokos Tis Anixis* is similar. There is something perpetually disturbing about experiencing the sudden repetitions that take hold in this work. The jolt from field recordings to digitized loops always seems unexpected and unfamiliar. Richard remarked to me that he learns to anticipate that looping will occur and listen out for it. This is an experience I have shared, yet I find the moments at which these will occur to be unpredictable. For me, it is this conflict between anticipation and unpredictability which creates a space that is active and charged. Richard has described this as one of the most alluring aspects of the work. The loops serve as stark reminders that what I am listening to is a digital recording of another time and another place, the immediate past reactivated into the immediate present and transformed in the process. The simple enchantment of listening passively to these beautifully recorded places is contrasted strongly with fissures and whirlpools that cut deeply into the immediacy of the environmental world.

Jennie sums up the experience of listening to this work beautifully when she says that:

> There is such a delicate balance here of carefulness and spontaneity, observation and intervention. It is work that lures you in with its surface and then keeps you riveted with the remarkable tightness of the generating ideas and their execution. I have the sense that everything is placed exactly in the right place, and that the whole project would fail without an incredible attention towards the smallest detail.

It is these details that are so alluring, and which encourage listening to become active. The natural environment becomes a piece of music and each sound an essential component of a composition. (After one close listening session, I stepped outside to hear a bird singing and was immediately drawn to the repetitions in a wholly different way to what I am accustomed to.) When listening to these recordings I become aware of the rhythm and repetitions of the natural world. Someone is chopping wood and the rain drips onto an old tin roof. Are these digital manipulations or untreated sounds from the environment? At times it is difficult to tell.

And then there are the loops themselves. Richard has said that there is an enormous difference in character between these; some very nuanced and others more startling. In particular, he remarked that the loops of shorter duration had more impact than the longer ones. For me, these aspects play an important role in how we perceive the work. There are times when the sonic environment almost seems to flip around; the processed loops continue for a length of time that is long enough for them to assume a certain normalcy. Breaking out of these repetitions and returning to the "natural" environment becomes uncanny, forcing the field recording to sound artificially manipulated. I recall having had a similar experience when watching the experimental films of Martin Arnold in which an obsessive loop has the effect of making the proceeding film footage seem stranger and more obscure than before. After experiencing these loops, one needs time to readjust to a more dialogical time.

Tsunoda writes that the number of loops can vary from 3 to 100. What is also varied is the degree to which these vary from one track to the next. It is almost as if Tsunoda is playing a perceptual game with the listener. I often find myself questioning whether a particular point in the recording is looping or not. In track 1, the manipulation is so frequent that the surface is kept alive and active, while on other tracks, the repetitions barely seem to register at all. Even in the tracks where repetition can be perceived with more frequency, I always find myself in a loop retrospectively. This is one of the most intriguing aspects of repetition, of course; one can only be aware of it once it has begun to happen.

Richard notes that Jennie's descriptions of shapes (triangles, circles, etc.) are an imaginative framing for the loops, adding that the 2D, or even 3D visualization brings in a spatial dimension that takes the description beyond merely that of their duration. Jennie's observations highlight for me how each loop has its own particular quality and dimension which can change over time. I was particularly drawn to her description of track 8 and the ways that different dimensions and qualities are revealed with each iteration. At another point in her commentary she mentions, "While I know it is impossible, during this repeated, wide-ranging loop my mind's eye pictures one bird slightly suspended, driving some type of machinery with a fierce call, while another somewhere above comments on the proceedings." This reminded me of my own listening experience—there are times when I imagine the environmental sounds continuing beneath the glitchy loop, as if the two things were existing simultaneously, forcing further the aforementioned aspects of perceptual disorientation.

Composer Michael Pisaro has remarked that this work presents an entirely radical view of time in music.[2] I would agree, in the sense that I find this work to be both elegant and intriguing in its reevaluation of the past and present, the natural and the artificial. It raises questions about the ways in which we perceive the world and our place within it.

Notes

1   Jonathan D. Kramer, *The Time of Music* (New York: Schirmer, 1988), 367.
2   Quoted in "O Kokos Tis Anixis (Grains of Spring)," http://www.soundexpanse.com/kokos-tis-anixis.

CHAPTER SIX

Monoliths: Laurie Spiegel's *The Expanding Universe* and André O. Möller's *musik für orgel und eine(n) tonsetzer(in)*

Jennie Gottschalk

The pieces I will be focusing on in this chapter have made me feel as if they began before the start of the track, and as if they do not end when they stop sounding. Their static harmonic frameworks ensure that even when exiting and returning to the piece, whether through proximity or degrees of attention, I find myself back in the same territory. Beyond that, when tones are drawn from a single harmonic series, the chords have a familiar, elemental quality. They are not foreign or unusual objects in themselves, but are derived from a familiar basis. Such a world is, for me at least, a very welcoming environment. The intense clarity of the harmonic series makes it plain to me in what world I am living. The rules of these worlds, the possible articulations and actions, become quickly apparent, and I am invited to find my own place within each of them.

It is challenging to sustain a discussion of a single work that has such similar properties throughout. There is a term that applies to this kind of task when it is approached in a subjective mode: it is a "meditation," in the sense of being an "introspective search."[1] This particular search has led me to think back on several moments in my own life to understand my relationship to one, and eventually two, works of music. My attempt to frame these moments from my own experience in chronological order came across as a very broken autobiography. They only assume coherence in relation to these listening experiences. What I hope to reveal here is a meditation on both how my images of these pieces have evolved, and on how my thoughts about it have reframed the experiences that surround it in my thinking. The chapter focuses on my experience of two pieces of music, but from that foundation extends outward to my history as a viewer and listener and its results.

One of my earliest tasks for this book was to pick two pieces to write about that had had a significant impact on me in terms of temporality. Tsunoda's *O Kokos Tis Anixis* was a clear choice for me, but I was unsure of the second piece. I kept remembering two listening experiences—of Laurie Spiegel's *The Expanding Universe* (1975)[2] and André O. Möller's *musik für orgel und eine(n) tonsetzer(in)*[3] (2003). I began by settling on the Spiegel example. I found, though, that for the same reasons that *The Expanding Universe* was so appealing to me, it was difficult to describe it with depth or clarity. Initially I even had trouble taking any notes on it at all. Compounding my concerns was the fact that I am not proficient with the technologies she used to make it, so I couldn't talk about it in terms of construction. This chapter is not intended to be about construction, but about my experience of the work. Still, my experience was so open and so ephemeral that I was at a loss. I felt good about my choice, though, because it is a piece that has had an interesting and memorable effect on me in terms of temporal perception, and it is also a direct contrast with the Tsunoda. Conversely to *O Kokos Tis Anixis,* it is not sectional, and it is completely unbroken. Tsunoda's piece has numerous irregular aspects of disorientation, whereas Spiegel's piece is consistently disorienting, or perhaps reorienting.

These problems seemed intractable, and eventually led me to question the "choose a single piece" premise of the initial discussion of each chapter in the book. But what could I compare it to? Spiegel talks about "slow change music."[4] For me, with my listening history, that evokes Éliane Radigue, André O. Möller, James Tenney, Catherine Lamb, La Monte Young, and others. I made a list and worked my way through it. I'll write about that series of encounters shortly, but first I will give a context for all of these encounters with a memory that took on new dimensions as I worked through them.

1984, Munich

When I was six years old, my family visited Germany and we spent some time at the Alte Pinakothek. I spent about fifteen minutes staring at *The Great Last Judgement*[5] (1614–17) by Peter Paul Rubens. My parents gave me plenty of space to have my own experience of it, but when I finally spoke with them about it, I said, "He had a really good imagination about hell, but he didn't have a very good imagination about heaven." Looking back at the painting now, though I see that it differs from my memory, the observation still feels more or less right—if a bit judgmental for a six-year-old. The focus of the entire scene is declared in the title, and it is not an equal division between heaven, purgatory, and hell. It is about judgment and separation, and not really about those select few who have gone upward.

While I can't fully account for my thoughts of over thirty years ago, I may know myself well enough to speculate that I was primarily voicing my sense of a missed creative opportunity. Heaven itself was not the premise of the work, but instead judgment, which is a highly turbulent scene. Heaven is conveyed in a small sliver of the painting. This depiction is incredibly pale and lifeless—both in background and in foreground—in comparison with the flailing nakedness of the lower part of the painting.

The people in the clouds are, with one exception, either standing around or looking down to see the action. No one is particularly interested in that environment. Everything behind the people in the foreground is muted—ultra-pale flesh tones and sun-drenched clouds, and a barely blue sky. The human figures in the background are so pale as to look almost blue. Those whose attention is not directed below seem bored, as well as boring. Below the clouds, everyone is painted in larger dimensions and in multiple vivid colors. Their flesh tones are brighter and more varied than the garments of their holier counterparts. They are the evident focus of the work. There are collisions, tensions, entanglements, and a range of distinct facial expressions. Without the action down below, there would be no action and no painting.

What could such a painting be if it were focused entirely on the top quarter of the action, on the actions and interactions of those who were neither watching nor participating in human misery? Knowing more of the world now, I feel a bit self-conscious asking that question, but I will still ask it on behalf of my six-year-old self. Could such a scene be colorful and interesting if it were not itself placed in contrast with the vivid forms, colors, and evocations of human agony? To do so, I guess I already knew on some level, would require a great deal of imagination. It's the kind of imagination I glimpsed in the work of Georgia O'Keeffe and Mark Rothko, and found more fully years later in Agnes Martin and Vaclav Boštik.

Several decades later, visual and sonic works that have a quality of uninterruptedness still have a special draw for me. The narrative functions of conflict and resolution, tension and release, play out in the news, in sports, in the arts. This is how the world seems to watch itself going on. When forces are in opposition, whether they are geological or political or personal, there is something to talk about in that friction. What happens when that friction has been removed? Apart from narrative, how can such a thing be made or discussed? This kind of music might deal with intensities and resonances. My best chance of talking about this work, I decided, would be to compare it with one or more other works that also deal with intensities, small events, and hues. By holding the works next to each other, I hope to compare their colors, their forms, their methods of variegation, and the differences—however subtle—in their effects on my sense of the passage of time.

It says something about the nature of these pieces, too, that they cause me to recall and ask new questions about an experience from my childhood. Their sense of scale is vast, and my sense of the temporality of my own experience seems to expand to meet that vastness.

Other pieces

I listened to many pieces that seemed related, but however significant they are on their own terms, there were differences in form, behavior, and impact that made them less applicable in this type of comparison. I learned a lot through this process, though, about the kinds of qualities that were essential to my experience of these two specific works.

James Tenney's approaches to both harmony and form seemed quite pertinent, and that led me to consider making *in a large, open space* (1994) one of the central pieces of the chapter. The works that would seem most likely to fulfill this sense of wholeness and unlimited duration would be installations, and one installation in particular. *In a large, open space* is harmonically static, built on the overtone series of a low F. The first thirty-two pitches of this series are laid out for each of twelve or more instrumentalists to choose from. The title is not just an image but an instruction that the piece is to be played in an open area, with musicians on the lower pitches concentrated toward the center of the area. The musicians move between pitches that are available both within the given series and on their instruments. Each pitch is played for "some 30 to 60 seconds." In selecting the next pitch, they avoid duplication both of their own previous pitch and whatever is being played by their neighbors. Change is occurring throughout, but it is slow and entirely irregular.[6] Though not written in the score, it is implied and has been a general practice that listeners can move throughout the space, experiencing the piece as a live installation.[7] Listener placement, pitch change, and overall duration are fluid. What remains fixed is the location of the musicians and the harmonic series in which they operate. This juxtaposition of fixed harmony and fluid reception seems perfectly aligned with the Spiegel and Möller examples, which also are built on single overtone series and afford a great deal of freedom in the listening experience.

But my actual experience of the piece was not anything like this type of immersion. At Bates Mill during the 2008 Huddersfield Contemporary Music Festival, the Bozzini Quartet performed at the center of a version of this piece. The audience, including myself, wandered around among the players and through the harmonic series. In retrospect, it felt like the listeners were as much on display to each other as the performers were to them. I was inhabiting a social situation, rather than a harmonic one. The sonic qualities and layout were secondary to the choices of how to physically navigate the space.

While I only have the memory of the piece, and haven't heard it recently, my recollection is that it did not have an overpowering effect. Moving through it became a question literally of location, and was very much a walking—rather than a swimming or floating—experience. Physically moving in space was difficult to map to harmonic positioning for me in that case, though I often imagine physical vistas and landscapes while listening to sound, and I do like to imagine these scenarios.[8] But I was not really sonically immersed in this piece. I was spatially immersed in it and could always hear some sound, but never in a way that affected my subjectivity such that my sense of the passage of time was transformed.

Spending some time with other Tenney pieces, I found that while the harmonic or formal profiles were a good fit, specific choices of instrumentation or configuration led away from the sort of immersive qualities I sought. But he's an important connecting figure for many of the people mentioned in this chapter, having worked with Éliane Radigue in New York in 1961 and worked at Bell Labs before Laurie Spiegel. He was also an influence on Möller.

I thought Catherine Lamb might have some work along these lines, in part because of her studies with Tenney, and also because of her extensive interest in tuning.[9] But her interest extends to shading, as demonstrated clearly in *matter/moving* (2011) and *in/gradient* (2012), and draws me as a listener away from a static experience as effectively as any developmental form. The beating patterns she sets up create clear patterns of tension and release. The movements away from a central tuning are slow, pronounced, and deliberate. Other pieces like *curvo totalitas* (2016) are more developmental and sectional.[10] Much of her work deals in shadings, in departures from an overall wholeness or totality that are so frequent that no such totality ever comes into view. There is a sense of change that she looks for, a sense of development or gradual refinement (see *in/gradient*), rather than an immersion in something that has always been.

I also spent some time with Éliane Radigue's work, settling on *Jetsun Mila* (1986) for a time, but it turns out to be highly sectional.[11] Each section could be taken in the terms I was looking for, but it felt important to me to look at entire unbroken worlds for this chapter, rather than works that involve shifts or lengthy transitions from one set of behaviors to another. Chuck Johnson has pointed out that in Radigue's work, "even with attentive listening it can be difficult to perceive structure."[12] And yet those shifts are present. She deals more in transitions and in sections than in monoliths.

I found that André Möller's *blue/dense* was also further from the type of listening experience I was thinking about than I had remembered, being more sectional than continuous in character.[13] In one listening session I wrote:

> Is this as relevant a piece as I originally thought? ... I find myself wanting to be temporally dislocated, but failing to be so. In part it's that I know the piece is sectional. The presence of human breath from time to time (heard in the onset) also pulls me back into measurable human time, although the lengths of the breaths are quite exaggerated with the technology that is used in the piece.[14]

Ultimately, its sectionality was what made it less relevant to the heart of this project than the organ piece.

Möller's *in memory of James Tenney* (2015) includes a piece subtitled "expanding universe."[15] I was struck by the similarity to Spiegel's title, and wrote to him to find out if the evocation was intentional. I found out that no, it was really just a coincidence. He didn't know this piece. The piece itself did not, as it turned out, have the type of impact on me that I was seeking based on the correlation of titles. But the image of an expanding universe, allied with a long swim in pitches derived from a single chord, seemed to be uniquely appropriate. Why?

Expanding universes

The sense that such a universe—whether it be musical or astronomical—could go on without interruption, not ever truly starting or finishing, seems fitting. It is allowed to expand. At the same time, it has certain gravitational pulls and principles, not only in its framework but in the set of available possibilities that can occur from one moment to the next. Does the universe itself expand, or do we become more aware of its dimensions over time? It is a speculative question, and impossible for me to answer outside of my own subjectivity.

What kind of temporal experience is suggested by an expanding universe? For me, it depends entirely on how grounded I am within it. If I am disoriented, lost, or confused, it's terrifying. On the other hand, to be trapped would also be terrifying. Those are two extremes that can make any duration—however brief—feel too long. But if it is grounded and rich and open to possibility, it can be an incredibly full and satisfying time, like entering into a new environment and taking it in with every sense.

In a musical context, small fluctuations, shifts in direction, and micro-events are constantly occurring, and they are all the more evident because other aspects of the work are so static. But a kind of inversion occurs as well, where the very slowness or stasis of harmonic, rhythmic, and timbral parameters allows me to enter into these spaces with a sense that it is, whether despite or because of its limitations, an entire open universe.

As I write this, I'm realizing that it's no coincidence that my website about experimental music is called Sound Expanse. My engagement with the field is one of immersion—spending time within it through listening, travel, writing, composing, interviewing, and so on to try to get a sense of this territory, how it operates, its hidden nooks and crannies, its boundaries. It is a field in continuous development and I will never know it entirely, but I can know it better through continued immersion.

Möller listening experiences (2015)

Writing about a great deal of music, as I did in *Experimental Music since 1970*,[16] involves listening to quite a bit more than is covered. As I worked on that project for over two years, a certain kind of saturation began to set in. It felt more difficult to sit back and listen to music. I was always trying to connect the dots, or else I was realizing that what I was hearing did not connect to my larger project. Works I was listening to became pieces in a puzzle. The puzzle will never be finished, but it felt important that connections be established with some semblance of clear logic. My listening process in general became very targeted and analytical.

When I put on André O. Möller's *musik für orgel und eine(n) tonsetzer(in)* (as played by Eva-Maria Houben at St. Suitbertus Church in Dortmund), this particular dot clearly fit, and quickly became a circle, a sphere, a world, a universe. It is still singular in its intent and in how it fit within the framework I was building; but it opened up a portal that enveloped me, providing a sonic and imaginative space that surpassed musical devices. It was totally engrossing and refreshing. I went on to listen to *blue/dense* (2003), which operated on similar principles but with different materials, and which had a related (though distinct) effect on me.

Spiegel listening experience

At a later point in the book-writing process, I was feeling similarly overwhelmed with the amount of sound work I was trying to consume and understand. I sat down to get a sense of this piece, and it seemed like it would be somewhat long. Somehow the half hour passed in a moment, and I knew that I had found something that reached me in a fundamental way. It seemed like a beautiful act on Spiegel's part to create such an open space. It offered an uninterrupted expanse, a careful balancing of absorbing foundational structure and complementary details. It absolutely merited close listening, and still does every time, but it doesn't reveal any devices. The techniques she used to make the piece at Bell Labs were extensive and laborious, but they led to something that sounds absolutely seamless and is part of an irreducible whole.

Zeroing in

So after exploring a number of other pieces by Spiegel and Möller, as well as the other aforementioned composers, I returned to these two memories of listening and the pieces that went with them. How was it that these two recordings had such a hold on my memory after several fairly turbulent years filled with a great deal of recorded music? What did they have in common?

The simplest answer is that they caused me to lose track of both clock time and physical place. In these instances, I found that I was not sitting down to complete a task of listening to a piece, but becoming immersed in an environment. I'll explain the similarities and differences between the pieces in the rest of the chapter, but for the moment I'll try to recall their direct impact on me at that time, which from the present moment is rather indistinguishable. I found that I couldn't take notes. It felt like there was too much to experience and the note-taking process would be nothing but an interruption. There also was no consistent temporal grid. When music listening becomes a task, it is a sort of default to watch the minutes go by on the CD counter, but I could not do that in either case. The immersive qualities of the music and the aperiodicity of the foreground caused me to completely lose track of time. In both cases, the end of the track was only apparent for musical reasons, because of some tapering. Temporally, it came as a total surprise. The two experiences were completely absorbing and restful.

Technically, the pieces have significant aspects in common. Both derive their entire material from a single harmonic series, and in fact are built on the same fundamental, or at least the same pitch class of C. They use extended sustained tones. (Spiegel also uses repeated tones, but sustained tones are almost always present.) Entrances and exits are not abrupt but tapered. Melodies are not constructed, but instead result from the interplay of overtones in a subtle shimmer. Foreground and background are not differentiated by type of material, but seem to be shifts in perspective from moment to moment. The degrees of presence and absence of sonic material are indicators of one's placement in the environment. The formal shifts are in density and range of material, rather than type of material. The properties of the musical material are consistent throughout.

The differences between the pieces can initially be described based on their surface aspects. *The Expanding Universe* was created at Bell Labs on a GROOVE console. It is early computer music, while Möller's piece is for organ. The timbres of the two instruments, as they are used here, are more similar than might be expected. Spiegel's piece is less than half the duration of Möller's, at 28:28 compared to his 73:44.

Before exploring the relationship between the two works in more detail, I'll write about the pieces and my experiences of them individually.

Laurie Spiegel: *The Expanding Universe*

Spiegel writes that the GROOVE hybrid system permitted "the creation, storage, editing, and manipulation of a piece of music as pure pattern change, over time, parameter by parameter. This [is] rather different from conventional musical notation, which records music on paper as descriptions of individual events, one by one."[17] This quote about the GROOVE system technology goes along with the total coherence of this sound space. We experience transitions of parameters, but not events as such. She continues, "Instead of pitch, amplitude, timbre, I had location, hue, value, saturation, texture, and the same time-structuring, storage, and editing capabilities."[18]

Part of this piece's appeal for me is that I don't understand how it was made. I am not versed in its technology beyond Spiegel's brief description of it. I don't have technical insights into the workings of the piece. Beyond that, its temporal impact is still somewhat mysterious to me. I can begin to outline reasons why it affects me as it does, but even after many listenings, writing sessions, and comparisons with other works that are historically or aesthetically relevant, there is still some mystery there. In fact I find that as I listen to the piece, I am resistant to writing about it in a narrative flow. I simply don't experience it as a passage of time.

I thought of it for a time as "vertical music," largely because of its firm roots in a single fundamental.[19] There might be something to that, but it doesn't resemble my more considered experience of it either, which is neither horizontal (development over time, unfolding melodies, etc.) nor vertical, but spatial. The closest imagined experience I can liken it to—one that becomes more vivid every time I hear the piece—is a listening tour of a galaxy. Everything is existent already, though not necessarily static. What is shifting is my position within the objects and events that are ongoing. Sound objects, pulsations, and mutual impacts advance and recede from my vantage point. The scope of the space I am occupying feels massive, but my perspective on it is changing very gradually and gently. It is an ungrounded, nondirectional experience of floating or flying among these objects. It doesn't feel like much of a stretch of my imagination to think of this work as an installation that has transcended the physical limitation of an act. My experience of it resembles that of a flight simulator or a description of travel in a book of fantasy or science fiction far more than a piece of music or a sound installation. Though of course I know that the inputs of the piece are reproducible (the CD track can be played any number of times), each time I sit down to listen I feel like my efforts to describe the event impede my experience of it. It's not so much a "blink and you miss it" concern, but rather that the mere grip on a laptop and the reference to its keyboard structure impede the suspension of disbelief that the piece brings about so powerfully.

The previous paragraph is in equal parts a description of the piece and an explanation of the relative sparsity of my notes on it. It might also be an attempt to describe the indescribability of the indescribable. That indescribable thing is the temporal experience of a work that overwhelms my sense of temporality. All that being said, I'll include several sets of listening notes below to relay some of the details of that experience.

May 22, 2017, listening session

It truly does feel like a universe built around one note, one massive, unbroken sustain. Harmonic series. Pulsations are wrapped into the sustain. I am made to feel at home here. It invites me to participate in its rhythms viscerally. At 5:20 I still feel that only a moment has gone by because the musical content has been shaping me rather than me marking time.

Differentiations in pulse. Have we traveled anywhere harmonically? Has the fundamental changed? Increasing number of sound objects. Pulses are more independent of the fundamental [not harmonically but in terms of their prominence], *but still essentially part of one body or environment.*

More bass. Rising tides around 19:30. Levels—undulations, pulses, crescendos. Marking time, expanding time, contracting time. When does it feel shortest/longest compared to what it actually is? How can I find this out?

June 24

Expanding through the harmonic series. The fundamental is the center, the point of gravity. Expansion of timbre and dynamics as well as pitch. Rhythms have suggestions of pulsation early on. At 3:40, the pulsation takes on a more prominent role.

There is a sense of sweeping through the possibilities, slowly, and gradually expanding what is possible. The rates of pulsations become more diverse. New parameters are being added. The pulsation rate starts increasing within one instance around 6:40.

The rules seem to be developing within the experience, rather than being externally imposed. The vibrations, pulsations, and strong harmonic profile makes me feel like something is bubbling up out of necessity.

Even when I've intended to, I find it very difficult to segment this experience into separate listening moments. It's [almost] a full half an hour almost but it is riveting every time.

The variations in pulsation rate are part of that: it never becomes known or predictable in its activity.

Increases in density [i.e., 10:45]. A growing number of active agents. The pulsations seem to have characters and behaviors of their own. The [harmonic] ground is stable, there is still gravitation, but all sorts of things are going on in this environment. I do picture it as action on a planet, impact on a living sphere.

Is there an under-over sort of construction? Fundamental and drone is under, pulsations over, pulsations are like weather events.

Rates are faster for higher-pitched tones.

June 28

Opens with exploration of harmonic series, fills in with expanded timbres, time is unmarked. It glides, rather than presenting abrupt shifts. Pulsations are first introduced around 1:30. The pulsations gradually (but rather quickly) become more active, occupying more pitch space. Pulsations are sometimes set against each other, each with a different pitch and rate.

I have the sense that the whole is always active, and it is only my perspective that is changing. This is much like the Tenney, in a large, open space. There is a principle, a fundamental, a basis for all this activity, and the pulsations are the detailed events within that clearly ordered space. What is known is the harmonic space. The prominence of one element over another, the audibility of a particular pitch and pulse rate, and its juxtaposition with other pitches and pulse rates are the details that become objects of focus.

What others may call a meditation, I think of as a realignment [layers, rather than transitions].

Around 18:46, there are more audible layers than heard previously. They coexist, interacting with each other only insofar as they don't obscure each other but simultaneously imprint themselves in the listening space.

July 1

The opening is a smooth transition through parts of the overtone series. There are no abrupt shifts but gentle introductions and transitions. Pulsations begin to reveal themselves, repetitions on single notes, as the most prominent change on the surface (from presence to absence and back). The timing of these pulsations is irregular, always a surprise—sometimes internally even, sometimes irregular, sometimes multiple pulsations are juxtaposed. The pitches are different each time. Meanwhile, there are smoother transitions of pitch and amplitude under that sonic surface.

This piece has a sense of timelessness. There is no single pulse but many pulses, fluid transitions between states, no clear arrivals or departures but a gradually expanding set of possibilities. I have the sense that I am not traveling to a different zone over time, but instead hearing more of what is happening within the zone we started in. It is a shift in hearing that happens over time, rather than a shift in perspective or position. Since there are no clear transitions from one space to another, but instead an occupancy of a single space, time is essentially removed from the range of consideration. It is a space to occupy.

What is this universe that is expanding? Is it utopian? Everything is always possible. This sound world is coherent throughout. The only jarring or abrupt thing would be a pitch/timbre/rhythm that came from outside of this set of possibilities. But once the world has been set up, however narrow the set of limits, anything possible within it can occur at any moment.

August 8

Everything is so grounded in one aspect that my entrance as a listener is into a single unfolding activity. There is no break in continuity, but the consequences of the given universe are becoming more apparent and intense. The vertical nature of this piece is not a by-product simply of a relationship to a harmonic series, but the quality of deepening a texture within a clear framework. When the pulsations begin, they are only a continuation of that sense of consequence and possibility within the given parameters. One thing is limited (harmony) but within that limitation it seems like there are an ever-expanding number of possible expressions. A pulsation and a sustain. Another sustain cross-cuts the pulsation. The notes present in the chord are shifting from moment to moment, though they are all on the same basis. There are clear aspects of foreground and background. The way these voices phase in and out is seamless. I can't tell when one begins and another ends. They seem to all be there always, and the clarity of appearance is a matter of perspective rather than presence. I am traveling through this network of possibilities, seeing more detail as I approach one thing more closely and others fade. My perspective is actually shifting from moment to moment, in the sense that something is always advancing or receding. There is a quality of weightlessness that takes me out of a temporal flow. The grounding is there, but I am traveling freely among its consequences. The grounding is of a network of possibilities rather than of me as a listener. Weightlessness here feels equivalent to timelessness. It's like swimming or what I imagine flying might be, a departure from the usual relation to ground. Everything is rounded, circular. There are returns, circlings back, things that glimmer and then recede. It is both simple and complex: simple in its limitation of possibilities, complex in its outcomes. Twenty minutes have gone by and it could as well have been five minutes or forty minutes, as far as how I am experiencing the work. The track began from nothing, but every possibility was embedded within the opening. I am witnessing these possibilities in an untethered way. It feels to me like a flight. I am not choosing the direction of the flight, but the things that come into and go out of focus are all within my realm of interest and might as well be of my volition. Rather than being (as it literally is) a fixed recording, it feels like a transcendent installation. It is like flying through an unknown, airborne ecosystem. At the close of the track, the view becomes more clear and I can see farther to some horizon. Perhaps it is a gentle exit from that space.

André O. Möller: *musik für orgel und eine(n) tonsetzer(in)*

André Möller describes the construction of this piece as follows:

> in this piece only those frequencies of the organ sound that have close to whole-numbered ratios (+/– 6 cents) to a fundamental (in this case C' at about 32 Hz). because the frequencies are never perfectly tuned – a result of the organ's tempered tuning – more or less strong beatings and frictions emerge, that rhythmically and timbrally shape the inner life of the sounds.[20]

I did not have as much trouble finding words to accompany this piece as I did with the Spiegel. My first complete listening in some time resulted in an essay of sorts, even with a twenty-minute lapse.

July 31, 2017, listening session

It starts without introduction, as if it has already been going on beforehand. [In retrospect, I'm not at all sure that this is even perceptually true. I wrote it down then but I think I had an agenda at the time. This comment is more relevant to the Spiegel.] *I can't tell if the overtones I'm hearing were there perpetually or if I am just noticing their presence after a short interval of listening. They seem to become more and more active, but they are still phantoms. It is a fleeting foreground of activity, as if some imp is working behind the scenes to play with my senses. Other, played notes become more prominent, also changing the contours of the half-audible motion. On the level of human articulation, nothing has changed. The same notes have been sustained. No tone has been added, removed, or even rearticulated. But there is a phasing in and out, and a resultant flickering of the harmonic components of the sound.*

Suddenly, around 5:30, new tones in the chord are added. I no longer hear melodies, but instead something like pulsars at a frequency not much higher than the added tones played on the organ. New low tones enter at 8:00. It feels like no time has gone by. Two and a half minutes normally feel to me like at least a modicum of time has elapsed, but the pace of change feels quite rapid at this point. The harmonics are going wild. It sounds like a whole string and brass orchestra busily creating an intricate texture. The level of activity is immense. And yet I know these are sustained tones only and their results. There is some change in registration around 10:45 that feels like an inundation of harmonic activity. What felt at first like a baseline of trackable activity has become an entire universe in itself, something that cannot be grasped in all its levels.

Just after 14:00, the weather becomes more turbulent. Sounds are blurring past each other, swirling in a chaotic hum. It is a total submergence, not just in a chord but in that swirl and all its harmonic consequences. It never seems to diminish, but always to increase. I feel like I'm in some sort of aural illusion equivalent to Escher's staircases that are perpetually rising while looping back on themselves. The harmonic activity might indeed be more complex over time, but the constantly changing weather patterns are at odds with the absolute grounding in a single fundamental and chord structure.

My sense of time passing is not linear. I am relating to this chord, this body of sound, in terms of depth of placement in a vast body of water. There are different patterns of motion, different levels of visibility. They do not unfold neatly over time. It is not a progression. It is a single volatile body with perpetually shifting temperatures and conditions. Rhythms occur as a by-product of those conditions, and not as accelerants in and of themselves.

Sometime around (or before) 25:00 I seem to lose my grasp on the specific conditions, lumping it all together as volatile and complex. It is no less absorbing, but just too hard to pick apart the micro from the macro level.

Around 27:50 it suddenly pulls back to something that I can observe more closely. It is a contained environment, or at least calmer waters. I am again listening for detail.

* * *

If I'm honest, I fell asleep. I woke up at around 48:00, and the waters were noticeably calmer. Lower tones have been removed. There are stirrings, but they are subtle and soothing, not vast and overwhelming. Contrary to what I'd expect, the continually diminishing (I'm at 55:00 by now) level of activity makes time seem to pass more quickly. I am not caught in the storm, but can relax and take in the wider vistas. I'm traveling smoothly on the surface of the water, rather than being in some relative sense of danger in the midst of it. That heightened sense of safety offers me a calmer space for reflection. I don't shut off at the spectrum of activity, but open myself up to its subtleties. I'm in a more receptive state, not at all restless, because this is a place I want to be. It feels impervious to the turbulence, for example, of American politics. I'm traveling instead to some sort of horizon, not knowing how the waters will continue to be so clear but somehow sure that they will be. (I don't recall from my last listening how the track ends, but the end is approaching.) The activity has been distilled into some almost singular *essential quality—though the fundamental, in the harmonic sense, is no longer audible. I am experiencing the effect of some underlying calming of conditions. The cause of it is almost certainly relatively simple (fewer and higher notes being played at a lower dynamic level), but the effect in the context of the work is staggeringly beautiful. There is less activity resulting from the played tones. The activity is smoother than a whisper, but no more prominent. A low whistle, perhaps. The horizon seems to be nearer than ever, but I am experiencing less of its amplitude. I know I am traveling in that direction though, it is totally clear. The piece has become linear, in its simple decrescendo. The surface activity is really a phantom now. I can't be sure that I'm hearing anything other than the played tones. But I remember them, and there are signs that they are still present. I am fascinated by that threshold, and pulled into a very close, attentive listening. The sound of my typing is an unwelcome interruption. I hear flickers only of that activity now, just before 70:00. Now I don't even know what I'm hearing, perhaps the air conditioning in the other room. I need to wait until the track ends to know for sure.*

It is done, disappeared without a trace. I was hearing nothing from the recording for the last minute or more. The feeling I had of being on the boat was taken away from me. Perhaps I was never on the boat, but traveling alongside it for a time, or grasping the side and slowly slipping off. It is apparent to me that it is still traveling toward that horizon, but well out of my sight now.

The piece is at first immersive, then to me it feels vertical and turbulent— quite the opposite of linear. Then it becomes linear in the sense of a gradual diminishment of amplitude and register, then liminal as it slowly recedes from audibility. How much of that is simply a factor of my capacity to understand, to process, to hear? How much of it is the work itself? And then what of that is simply me and my reaction, and what is a by-product of normal bands of human perception? I will wait to learn more from others who have heard the piece. Listening again two weeks later, I came to an important—and seemingly obvious—realization about the form of the piece.

August 13

It opens with a single sustained tone, but many other tones are included among the overtones and there is a flickering in prominence between them. There is a slow timbral shift in the lowest (played) note, similar to a gradual vowel change in overtone singing. I know that a burst of sound in at least two new, prominent notes will come at some point but forgetting when builds up suspense. (My computer is charging in the other room so I don't have access to my notes.) The overtones are stirring, alternating, generating more suspense. Since other parameters are static, I am able to focus in behind the surface of the drone.

Here is the new entrance; new played notes make the overtone activity *more intense, alternating and flickering. As much of a surprise as those notes were the first time, as much as they built up suspense, they very quickly (in less than a minute) have become integrated into the texture in my listening experience.*

Now there are more low notes, the lowest yet, and the texture of the overtones, the alternating and flickering in prominence, is starting to go wild. More high notes (played) are quickly added, and the overtone activity is so rapid that it is no longer trackable but is instead a texture, very rapid streams of melody within tight registral areas. It is a great stirring.

I need to turn the volume up because I feel like I'm not fully in it. I see that all that I've narrated has happened at least eight minutes earlier, by 12:00. A long sustain with all that has accumulated with occasional additions. Unlike my sense of the pulsations in the Spiegel, a total environment or weather system has built up that is not composed of isolated events, but is an encompassing atmosphere. Occasional gusts might be new keys of the organ sustained, but I'm not sure. They don't seem to go away, but get wrapped into the texture. There is a certain rhythm of pulsation that dominates and feels very much equivalent to my own bodily rhythms, but I couldn't say which ones—breathing, pulse, and so on. There are many rhythms going though, and they are not in lock step. The rhythms are being controlled by the harmonic interactions.

A prominent entrance of a pitch class some octaves above the fundamental feels like a defining moment shortly before 23:00. New melodies are created by it. A chord is played around 24:00. It feels like we're coming to a formal demarcation. It's not particularly that the material is stretched out. It actually needs this much time to reveal itself. There is plenty of activity, plenty of change to keep me fully engaged, and even at times overwhelmed. The changes are so far all of a certain nature but they have a complex series of consequences in harmony and resultant rhythm.

The texture suddenly pulls back shortly before 28:00. I know what to be listening for, the pulling away and reappearance of the overtones, a kind of stirring or flickering (or perhaps a shimmering as a result of stirring,) and it is vivid and very present for me. Or I am present for it. At 30:30, the played notes are beginning to advance in front of the overtones, then recede again as I become more accustomed to them. The rate of shimmer is becoming faster and I don't know why or how. Now the shimmer is clearly in the foreground. The texture has not changed, but it has acted on me. What is the subject-object relationship here? It feels like the piece is playing me over time. Gradual changes have a lasting impact on what I hear and how I hear it. Harmony morphs into rhythm. Overtones become melodies. Foreground becomes background and vice versa.

There is a reduction in forces leading into 37:00. The shimmer is gradually stilling. There is motion but it has significantly slowed. Fewer elements are in motion as there are fewer played tones, but with each reduction there is still plenty of material to listen to. It would be fascinating to listen back to this section for absence, trying to hear what's going away with each instance of removal. A high, almost rattling sound becomes apparent through reduction of more prominent melodies (43:00). Other rhythms develop too, even as there seems to be an almost-complete diminishment in texture. I can't really tell at this point which notes are being played. Maybe it's a lowish note that began the piece. Is there a second one? Third? There must have been three because something went away and now it sounds like at least two. We're back at the calm surface of the water. Fewer things are flickering. For a moment I thought there was stasis, but then I heard something else. In any case it feels calmer than before, though change is still rapid in the reduction of elements.

The return to a single note feels like something to anticipate as much as the original anticipation of the higher chord. That felt like an age ago. This reductive process is lengthy in time. (It started at about 28:00 and is now still going at 50:30) but continually engaging, now still at 53:30.

There are compelling rhythmic changes even when there seems to be no change in played notes. I don't know how that happens. It is still reducing at 59:00. This is a momentous, compelling reduction. I can see how it allowed for sleep before but there is plenty to listen for in absence and presence. It feels like a total calm, the bluest of skies with no clouds or interference. Now I'm floating on the water looking upward. It is still diminishing at 63:00, yet still very present, still and peaceful, but clearly it feels like daytime and not nighttime. Different objects come into prominence, advance and recede within a vast expanse, without distinct temporal markers. For this moment, past and present feel indistinguishable. The end of the piece is somewhere on the horizon, and gradually the chord diminishes to nothing.

Having completed this closer and more careful listening, the entire form of the work has finally come into view. From 0 to 27:46, it builds. From that point to the end, it recedes. It seems fairly evident now that everything before this crest is an addition and everything after is a reduction, but I was caught up in moments rather than structure in earlier encounters and didn't know that until this late moment. Formally, it mirrors James Tenney's, having never written a note for percussion (1971). It could almost be said to be that piece transcribed for organ. (But of course it isn't.) The clarity of the form is something that recedes into the background, allowing various harmonic and perceptual phenomena to come into clear view.

Conclusion

Now that I've finally talked about the actual content and my listening experiences of these two pieces, I can address the question of differences between them. My memory of much earlier listening experiences had a nearly identical impact on me, both viscerally and temporally. The timbral and harmonic content, taken as a whole, is in fact rather similar between them. But the treatment of material, from foreground elements through to the overall form, is vastly different. Now that I know the pieces better, they are quite distinct experiences.

Spiegel's piece operates in some ways as an unordered list. A certain number of actions are possible (though at a number of pitches, speeds, and amplitudes) and can be brought in at any time. Things go in and out of focus in the listening experience, but there is an ongoing sense that all of them are always there. My perceived shift from moment to moment is in perspective, rather than in content.

In the Möller, the structure is additive and then subtractive. It begins with a single low tone, adds a note or two at a time, along with the resultant overtones, mounting to an incomprehensible complex of pitches, melodies, and rhythms all derived from these sustained organ tones. Then the pitches are slowly removed. The perceptual results of this process are so complex, and take place over such a long stretch of time, that it was far from obvious to me for some time how very straightforward the form was.

How then, given the basic formal differences between the pieces, do the perceptual experiences of them differ? Here I'll write from the standpoint of my later listenings, having more information. In the Spiegel, I am witnessing sound objects advancing and receding, and I am registering their appearance and disappearance from moment to moment much as I might with visual objects. In the Möller, I am anticipating. At the opening I anticipate the abrupt appearance of two notes in the organ. Then I am listening for more tones and their interactions. When the space becomes perceptually saturated, I keep imagining that the texture is one or two note-removals away from silence. Every removal leaves more than I expected until the very last actual moments of the piece. The image I returned to several times is a slow return to the surface of the water.

Though the processes of building up and reducing chords on the organ might objectively seem to be mirroring each other, they have very different perceptual impacts on me. Even with repeated listenings, the build evokes questions of what can occur within this world, while the removal makes me wonder what my position is within it. In terms of that imagery, the second part of the piece is more similar to the Spiegel than the first. There is no technical justification that I'm aware of for its greater degree of similarity, but the sense of a shift in position or perspective, rather than a shift in actual activity, is perceptually significant for me.

Lucy Lippard wrote of Ad Reinhardt's works that they were "empty stages upon which the observer could act out his own interpretive fancies."[21] Are there formal justifications for the differences between my fancies of these two pieces? Harmonically, they are both made of a single type of material.

They are monochromatic in that sense, though it could be argued that the use of overtones is equivalent to exploring hues of a color, rather than the color itself. Within my "fancy" of the Möller as an oceanic experience and of the Spiegel as space travel, I am no longer imagining myself to be on solid ground with the usual indicators of the passage of time. In the absence of harmonic change, my sense of temporality is fluid to the behaviors of other parameters such as rhythmic shifts and pitch additions—within the given harmonic structure—which help to steer the imagery, but do not create cuts.

That word "cut" is perhaps what I've been looking for all along.[22] There is no cut in either of these works. Even the point when the Möller goes from an additive to a subtractive process feels like part of a single flow, and is only definitely understood as a shift in retrospect. Spiegel writes that "slow change music" in this piece, "instead of being built by accretion of many individual musical events to form a texture, works by allowing the listener to go deeper and deeper inside of a single sustained texture or tone." The ear is no longer "on guard," and can "relax its filters."[23] *The Expanding Universe* operates from moment to moment, as an unbroken journey among interrelated objects. Möller's *musik für orgel und eine(n) tonsetzer(in)* is structurally directional, but perceptually similar in the surface level events that unfold through the interactions of tones. As tones interact with each other and with the environment, various events come into the perceived foreground and background. Perhaps the congruence in my thought between the pieces (despite their very different constructions) is a result of the perceived subtle advancing and receding surface elements in the midst of a reliably consistent structure. There are innumerable meaningful encounters with these surface details.

In two different ways, these works have thorough structural integrity: the Spiegel through the presentation of strongly related materials and the Möller through an ordered, yet variegated, presentation. The richness of material within those evident constraints is simultaneously (1) the thing that drew me to them, (2) formally challenging to describe, and (3) the source, for me, of a sense of being installed into a world that operates according to its own logic and sweeps me along with it. In my early notes on both pieces, I said that there was no narrative to unfold. Having lived with them longer, I now question that. The narrative is self-constructed—constructed by me. In each case, it is a visualized and viscerally experienced journey through an environment, observing the shifts in perspective and changes in conditions that occur along the way.

My first attempt to write this chapter involved starting with a chronological narrative of experiences I had that came back into memory as I worked with these pieces. That structure ended up feeling quite inappropriate to the material. Neither the pieces nor my experience of them are relatable as narratives, but as gravitational objects with expanding peripheries. The writing of this chapter has created a dynamic interaction between these two works and my own consciousness. The memories and associations I bring to these works expand their power for me, not only as disorienting temporal experiences but as meditations on my own most persistent gravitations. Each time I play one recording or the other, the content is apparently the same, but the journey is different every time. The repeated traversals of these territories point me back toward my own sense of self. For me, that is perhaps the clearest trait of their nonlinearity. In their explorations of defined harmonic and timbral spaces, they shed unexpected light on my own inner life. I am as surely a child as an adult as I become more awake to their qualities.

Notes

1   *Stanford Encyclopedia of Philosophy*, s.v. "meditation," https://plato.stanford. edu/entries/medieval-literary/#MedSol
2   Laurie Spiegel, *The Expanding Universe*, Unseen Worlds, UW09, 2 compact discs.
3   André O. Möller, *musik für orgel und eine(n) tonsetzer(in)*. Edition Wandelweiser Records, EWR 0702, 2007, compact disc.
4   Spiegel, *Expanding Universe*. Liner notes, 19.
5   See "*The Great Last Judgement* (Rubens)," https://en.wikipedia.org/wiki/ The_Great_Last_Judgement_(Rubens)
6   The one-page score is available at http://www.frogpeak.org/unbound/tenney/ InALargeOpenSpace.pdf?lbisphpreq=1.
7   This was true in the performance I witnessed in Huddersfield, others I have heard of in Chicago and Los Angeles, and is also evident in the video of a 2016 Montreal performance available at https://www.youtube.com/ watch?v=GM9PV0Gd_Nw.
8   I would like to experience and compare the live, spatialized events of pieces by Robin Hayward, including *Stained Glass Music* (2011) and *Tetrahedron* (2011). The conception is similar, but the harmonies are based on extended just intonation rather than the more generally understood harmonic series. The geometries of the space are designed to represent aspects of the harmonic relationships between pitches. In *Tetrahedron*, Hayward writes, "Having established an essentially static relationship between harmony and space, the composition focuses on moving through this space over time." See http://www. robinhayward.de/eng/comp/stainglass.php and http://www.robinhayward.de/ eng/comp/tetrahedron.php.
9   See http://sacredrealism.org/catlamb/tuninginformation/main.html.
10 Lamb's scores are listed at http://www.sacredrealism.org/catlamb/works/ listofworks.html.
11 Éliane Radigue, *Jetsun Mila*, Lovely Music, LCD 2003, 2 compact discs.
12 See http://www.chuckjohnson.net/wp-content/uploads/Empty_Music.pdf.
13 André O. Möller, *Blue/dense*. Edition Wandelweiser Records, EWR 0411, 2005, compact disc.

14 Author notes, August 2, 2017.

15 André O. Möller with Hans Eberhard Maldfeld, *in memory of James Tenney*. Edition Wandelweiser Records, EWR 1503, 2015, compact disc.

16 Jennie Gottschalk, *Experimental Music Since 1970* (New York: Bloomsbury, 2016).

17 Spiegel, *Expanding Universe*. Liner notes, 4.

18 Ibid., 5.

19 Jonathan Kramer writes about vertical time and the "eternal now" in chapter 12, "Time and Timelessness," in *Time of Music* (New York: Schirmer, 1988), referencing both psychoanalytical and musical thought.

20 Möller, *musik*. Liner notes. See also http://www.wandelweiser.de/_e-w-records/_ewr-catalogue/ewr0702.html.

21 Cited in Francis Colpitt, *Minimal Art: The Critical Perspective* (Seattle: University of Washington Press, 2010), 31.

22 For a greater understanding of this term in relation to both music and Gilles Deleuze's thought, I'm indebted to Christoph Cox's introductory workshop to his book, *Sonic Flux: Sound, Art, and Metaphysics* (Chicago: University of Chicago Press, 2018), at the 2017 Subtropics festival in Miami.

23 Spiegel, *Expanding Universe*. Liner notes, 17. Also see http://retiary.org/ls/expanding_universe.

Postlude to Chapter Six

Richard Glover

Along with discussion of the two pieces, Jennie's *Monoliths* chapter includes autobiographical accounts from different points in her life, which feed through, in various different ways, to her listening experiences of the two pieces. This inwardly reflective consideration of her own background and how it informs her listening provides a wide array of connections and relationships at play in the exploration of her own temporal experiences.

Jennie at one point wrote that both the Spiegel and Möller cause her to lose "both time and myself," describing how in Spiegel's *The Expanding Universe* it seems that "everything is existent already" and there are "no arrivals or departures," which was an aspect both Bryn and I experienced; I felt as if I was stepping into a texture which did not just begin when I started listening to the track, but had existed for much longer beforehand. The repetitions or waves, of new pitches, feel like decays of something already existing—echoes of some sort, but not something of which I would be able to identify the source.

As the track progresses, these decays become more like appearances of pulses as they follow a predictable regularity in their dissipation of dynamic. To me, these pulses interwoven with dynamically transitioning sustained tones provide a continual temporal tension: when they are layered, polyrhythms emerge and I experience two distinct temporalities pulling at each other, the forward propulsion of the pulses against the more glacial cyclical shifting of the sustained tones. It is not an unpleasant experience; it is part of the detail of Jennie's "shifting of position within the objects and events that are going on." I seem able to reside in between, or toward one or the other, of coexistent temporalities; as there is no clear linearity in the piece for me on the global scale, I remain entirely open to experiencing these different temporalities. Bryn commented that he experienced changes in the temporal flow throughout, but without points of segmentation. There are no obvious moments, either as experienced or in recollection, where significant auditory events took place; rather, the temporal flow changes from these continual "puddles" of decays.

Whenever I felt like the sound was expanding through an increase in textural layers, dynamic, or new pitches for the pulsations, the temporal flow began to rush out in front of me as if I was lagging behind the movement of the music, and I experienced a heightening of pace and activity. However, no sooner was I consciously aware of this change, then that expanding sound would quickly begin to ebb away. I was sustained, caught, within this world of expansion and contraction from the sonic characteristic, but as this continued on throughout the piece, this awareness of the constraining motion on the expansions itself began to drift away, toward a more heightened awareness of the expansiveness, or the "untethered" nature of the music, as Jennie states. Where she describes the listening experience as feeling like a flight, I sense the decaying pulses as clouds, changing within the vastness of a climate governed by its own rules.

There is notably little mention in Jennie's, Bryn's, or my own comments, of Spiegel's own stamp or directedness involved within the creation of the music; it seemed to prompt in all of us an inward reflection upon our own experience, and an awareness of subjective, inwardly *controlled* exploration. Spiegel is providing the necessary platform which motivates us to examine the limitations of our own temporal perceptions.

Bryn states that he can observe change, rather than having to look for it—change happens at a rate that is audibly perceptible, rather than having to be understood retrospectively. This perhaps supports the sense of unending expansiveness of the track, which is that it could stretch out indefinitely; there cannot be a clear endpoint where the track would stop—even though of course the track does stop, or rather we finish listening to the expansiveness—at 28:28.

As Jennie's comments about her listening for this piece are described in visceral, often visual, imagery, I understood her writing as more of a single short, but highly detailed and rich, transmission of data—many continuous streams of words, sentences, full of meaning for a reader to find and draw associations themselves, in one motion. I could envisage the track itself being a heavily time-stretched version of a one-second sample, and we are hearing all the resonances of that initial audio—with its expanse for us to explore, to fly through—in much the same way that Jennie's writing on *The Expanding Universe* provide many metaphors, images, and concepts which resonate long after I read them.

Möller's *musik für orgel und eine(n) tonsetzer(in)* provides a fascinating counterpart piece to discuss in Jennie's broader exploration of expansion and monoliths. Its opening section is much more imposing than *The Expanding Universe*, perhaps by actually having less movement. There are no composed elements which provide any transformation in the temporal flow outside of the expansion/contraction of the chord every few minutes, but as Bryn comments, "I am carried along its continuum"; I sensed waves arising from the harmonics, and this suggests to me more of a clear linear continuum, rather than the rhizomatic, "untethered" floating in *Universe*. Once the first clear change is heard, at 5:30, there is then immediately a sense of anticipation, of leaning forward, of a temporal experience which pulls me along and heightens my awareness of the perceptual present. It is extraordinary for me to contemplate that a piece with far, far less motion actually built into its construction than *Universe*, has a much greater sense of direction, of clarity in its teleology, and all-encompassing expansion.

This addition of a higher chord at 5:30, and the others which follow over the entire duration of the piece, provide clear points of segmentation in the piece, providing a distinctly different temporal flow to the Spiegel. Bryn points to the odd dichotomy that exists between stasis and motion here—he anticipates change, but the surface of the sound does not move, a reversal of sorts experienced in Feldman's *Piano, Violin, Viola, Cello*. This is music built out of slowness, ground almost to a halt—change is anticipated and observed retrospectively, and this all results in a more directed temporal flow, far removed from the minimal expansion/contraction compositional approach of the Möller.

The wide registral range of the organ chords were at times overwhelming, but Bryn felt this enabled a heightened focusing upon different aspects of the chords, rather than a need to continually absorb the entirety of the sound. Jennie remarks on the enormity of the sound which enveloped her. Bryn describes a sound which fills every nook and cranny of one's aural space.

Bryn commented upon the organ chords as seeming to be discovered, or emerging from, the instrument itself; this gave the linear directedness of the listening experience to *musik für orgel* an additional impetus, as if the sound was itself growing, expanding organically from the initial low tones. This provided a significant contrast to the studio production of *Universe*, in which specific pitches and motions were selected to be superimposed on one another, without the same kind of organic development of *musik für orgel*.

From 27:45 of *musik für orgel*, as the contracting structure of the second half becomes clear, Bryn notes that the removal of certain elements from the chord reveals other harmonies; his wanting to revel in these sounds is checked by the strong anticipatory nature of the structure, and the temporal flow which extends forward in a similar way as the early expansive structure did at the beginning of the piece.

There is then an inevitability about the dying away of the music at the end of the duration; this has been so clearly described to us already that I anticipate its occurrence and become aware of my expectations being fulfilled; at this moment, on a low single tone with few organ stops out, the temporalities experienced throughout seem to vanish into a wide expanse, as I am left wondering what comes next. When all expectations have been so fully delivered, how can we anticipate a future?

CHAPTER SEVEN

Observations on Musical Behaviors and Temporality

While the previous chapters have examined the temporalities of individual musical works, there is something to be gained by drawing on that series of observations from a wider angle. In this chapter, we will stay focused on the same set of pieces, but we will contemplate the musical traits and behaviors within them that we deem to have had the most significant impact upon us as listeners. Our observations remain specific to these works and to our own individual experiences of them. However, zooming out to the perspective of musical behavior will allow us to address some key aspects of musical construction. We are able to do so in this chapter by drawing on our earlier chapters, postludes, and from an extended conversation we had after writing our chapters and postludes; many passages in this chapter are quoted from that dialogue.

What all of the chosen works have in common is that we each experienced some kind of temporal disorientation while engaged in the act of listening to them. We wrote in some detail in the chapters about the nature of that disorientation and in the postludes we contemplated how it varied from one subject to another. In this chapter, we will try to identify the musical features within the works that caused the various types of disorientation that we experienced. We have found that these musical behaviors, taken collectively across the works, cover a wide range of parameters. In Feldman's *Piano, Violin, Viola, Cello*, the play with memory was effective through the use of slightly shifting surface patterns, paired with the long duration. The long duration of Möller's *musik für orgel und eine(n) tonzetser(in)*, combined with the slowness of its shifts in texture, distracts from the clarity of its form. The lack of directionality in Spiegel's *The Expanding Universe* is in itself disorienting, in that time cannot be effectively marked over a duration with so little change. Szlavnics' *Gradients of Detail* uses both shifts in form and prominent silences to create a sense of dislocation. The shifts in Tsunoda's *O Kokos Tis Anixis* from recording to loop, and in the scale of one loop to another, cause frequent shifts in each of our senses of temporal flow. In the Saunders, the many different and brief iterations of what is essentially presented as the same work create a challenge to a sense of perspective. In Ikeda's *+/–*, frequency (pitch) and speed of articulation were disorienting in a way that was inherent to its technological mode of sound generation.

This chapter inverts the process of the prior chapters, in which we started from the basis of the works themselves. Here, we will discuss the musical behaviors, the driving forces of temporal dislocation, though always from the point of view of being listeners to these particular works.

Form, structure, memory, and repetition

Bryn Harrison

The pieces selected in the previous chapters illustrated a range of approaches to musical form and structure that impacted in different ways on our senses of musical temporality. Most notably, each of the eight tracks under consideration showed differing tendencies toward continuity and discontinuity. While pieces such as Laurie Spiegel's *The Expanding Universe* and André O. Möller's *musik für orgel und eine(n) tonsetzer(in)* offered a clear sense of structural continuity throughout in which each sound merged into the next, Szlavnics *Gradients of Detail* and Feldman's *Piano, Violin, Viola, Cello* contained juxtapositions of materials (including—in the case of the Szlavnics—those between sound and silence) that provided immediate structural divisions in time. The different temporal perspectives that such approaches afford are complex and become even more so when one considers the behaviors of the materials themselves. While it is not possible to provide a comprehensive analysis of these tendencies here, we will offer some observations on the nature of the relationship between materials and structure in each piece.

We began our discussion by comparing the sense of time passing in the two pieces that Jennie discussed: Spiegel's *The Expanding Universe* and Möller's *musik für orgel und eine(n) tonsetzer(in)*. Although both pieces exhibit a clear sense of continuity in which a single expanse of sound is stretched to great proportions, we found that each composer carried the listener through their work in an entirely different way. It was observed that the arch-form of the Möller, which works on the principle of the gradual addition and eventual removal of musical material, provided a predictable structure for the listener, whereas the Spiegel avoided the notion of accrual and, as a result, felt like an all-enveloping space:

Richard: The Möller, I think, has got the most, after a certain time period, easily predictable structure, and then on reflection, by far the clearest form … Once you're familiar with the structure, it's like you're actually hearing time play itself out. And then I then thought about the Spiegel. That seems so different.

Jennie: Yeah, sort of atemporal.

Bryn: I think both you [Richard] and I commented on the fact that in the Spiegel, it's almost like everything is already there. And I think, Jennie, you said something similar when you said it almost seems to exist as an environment or a place …

Jennie: That sounds like me.

Bryn: Yeah, and I think it's interesting, because, with the Spiegel, it's so much based on the harmonic series that you almost become aware of the fact that all of the sounds that emerge or expand were already present. So it's almost like you're expanding *into* rather than *out of* something. You're almost aware that the journeying is towards something that was already there. Whereas I think with the Möller, you get the sense almost of an additive and subtractive process. …. You're waiting and you're anticipating for that next entry or exit of sound. And then it has this very clear arch form. So it carries you forwards, almost like a sort of projection of time. Whereas for me with the Spiegel, it's more of a kind of immersion into time itself, or into this kind of expansive world that somehow exists outside of some kind of agency of time.

It is apparent that becoming aware of being able to correctly anticipate a structure provided a very different sense of temporality to that of feeling at a loss to predict short-term outcomes.

After making these observations, we continued to compare the surface qualities of these two works more closely. As Jennie had identified in her chapter, both pieces were based upon the harmonic series from a fundamental tone. We went on to discuss the similarity of these surface aspects but also the ways in which these were perceived differently due to the different approaches to musical form:

Jennie: One thing I was thinking about is maybe more of a meta theme, rather than a specific musical quality: The idea of the surface aspects of the work versus what they're actually performing temporally. So for me, the Spiegel and Möller, though they're very different in form, are quite similar in surface aspects. They were based on a harmonic series, and they were immersive, at least for me. They both were places to me: places to occupy. You know where you are in terms of the harmony; but then because of the form, they actually operate very differently. And for all my efforts to find a piece to relate to the Spiegel, the two pieces end up being practically

            opposite in terms of clarity of form. I don't think I ended up
            saying that in my chapter.

Bryn: It illustrates to me that we don't just listen to harmony on the
            vertical, that you can't have harmony without the horizontal
            as well. And especially with the Möller, there's this real sense
            of listening through that piece, I think.

Richard: I agree with that word "projecting," Bryn. It's interesting
            that the Spiegel, on the surface, has—in terms of the amount
            of composed sounds—more activity. There is far more in
            the Spiegel, and yet it's the Möller, because of the structure,
            that to me seems to have much more movement … as if the
            intensity of those chords are pushing me forwards. Even
            though, from a very kind of basic construction level, there's
            far more going on in the Spiegel. I think I'm slightly more
            reticent to talk about the harmonic series in the Spiegel,
            because you don't know, especially the first time you hear it,
            what the pitches are going to expand out to be, so you don't
            know quite what the harmonic world will be, in which the
            piece is going to remain. It's only by remaining in it that you
            find out. On reflection, you can see what happened. I feel like
            it's a very specific kind of listener that would come in and be
            able to recognize at some point that it's a harmonic series.

Bryn: I remember hearing fundamental tones from which other,
            higher partials emerge and subside, and then I'm not quite
            sure how that relates to the beating patterns. But for me,
            those beating patterns … it's almost surface incidents within
            this world in which we inhabit, whereas I actually heard
            the onsets on the Möller really strongly. Like you can hear
            somebody depressing another key on the organ. Whereas
            with the Spiegel, because it's created in a studio, you're in this
            immersive environment.

Paradoxically then, we found that the Möller offered a greater sense of
projected motion despite exhibiting a lower level of surface activity. Each
arrival of a new note or chord became a structural marker from which we
were able to predict the onset of the next event. As Jennie discussed in her
chapter, each onset pulls us back into a measurable time.[1]

We observed that such tendencies are also evident in the Szlavnics. Despite
its lack of formal structure or harmonic grounding, there are distinct points
of arrival and reconciliation, which carry the listener forward to the next
event. We witnessed the ways in which the extensive use of glissandi guided
us toward these arrival points and discussed the ways in which the relative
proximity of pitches meant that some lines had further to travel to reach
their arrival points than others. The lack of harmonic stability meant that
one could only follow and, by following, reach these points of arrival which
acted as structural markers. Richard, in his chapter, talked about forward

momentum and the ways in which changes of density would seem to bring attention to changes in pacing. The title of his chapter, "Separation and Continuity," also makes reference to the prevalence of silence in the piece. As Jennie identified, there are nine silences in total. These are often of prolonged length and serve to break the otherwise continuous flow of materials into clear structural divisions. As Jennie noted, Szlavnics herself has spoken of her interest in presenting "clear structural forms."[2] These silences, however, do not appear to draw attention to the structure of the work itself but serve to heighten our concentration on each event as it occurs.

Such aspects are also at play in Feldman's *Piano, Violin, Viola, Cello*, which, similarly, is constructed from sequences of events and does not follow an observable pattern or adhere obviously and perceptually to the principles of causality. For all of us, the way in which the piece was put together was wholly disorienting and we discussed the confusion that arises from the unpredictable ordering of events. As with the Szlavnics, we found that the sense of musical anticipation that arises within the materials is counteracted by the fact that the overall structuring of events avoids any kind of internal logical that would provide a more pervasive sense of large-scale teleology. The resultant space that the listener occupies might be seen as somewhat different to the environment of the Spiegel discussed previously; in the Feldman, we can identify clear changes in pacing and the sense of being "carried through" from one moment to the next, but ultimately we lose track of where we are and must submit to the moment. Each internal local-level repetition magnifies the materials while simultaneously asserting that, being a repetition, it can never be exactly the same thing as that just heard. At the same time, each larger-scale structural repetition reminds us that that our perception of each is contextually dependent upon those that precede it.

Such considerations led to a broader discussion on the role of transformation and change in these works and their relation to memory:

Richard: I'm interested in the idea of which of these pieces have prompted changes, or transformation, from the way you listen or the way that you perceive temporality the most. Part of my impetus for this book came from reading an analysis of a sustained tone piece over an extended duration which simply stated what the materials were at different points in the track. And I think if you listen to a piece like that, the way that you listen has changed quite significantly by the end of the track, and at various points throughout. But I don't think that's just a duration, and I don't think it's as simple as "the longer the piece, the more you change." There are lots of variables, but I think some of those variables, we might be able to talk a bit more about. And we've got this nice range of very different pieces here, and I'm wondering if we can compare the idea of the amount of transformation, or whether you feel like—

Bryn: Isn't it to do with memory?

Richard: I think definitely that's part of it, yes. It's suggesting that it's
           like tracks that you listen to one day and then the next day.
           The next section starts at 22 minutes in, and it has a kind of
           low drone. And I think, as you say, it's not accounting for
           what happened. But more than memory, or at least memory
           being a big, expansive network of different things, having
           been pushed towards listening in a different way perhaps.

Bryn: Yes. But to give another example, it's the way that people talk
           about repetition in analysis, as if the second repetition is the
           same as the first repetition, and the third repetition is still the
           same as the first repetition.

Richard: That's the same thing, absolutely.

Bryn: Yes. Or like an ABA form, we get the recapitulation of the
           first material. Well, yes, in some ways it is, but the experience
           of listening to that for the second time is entirely different.
           Yeah. There was something I think I wrote in the Feldman
           chapter about a sort of paradox coming into play, that we
           have to focus on each moment, and yet there's no opportunity
           to reflect. And yet somehow embedded within that is the
           whole history of what we've heard. And all of that impacts
           immediately upon that moment. So for me, the Feldman, just
           to go back to—What was your point again, Richard? Were
           there some pieces that—

Richard: Prompt more change. Part of that change could be to do with
           reflection, and part of it might then be to do with suddenly
           shifting you into a different space in some way, say.

The point being made here was that any kind of musical analysis that draws
primarily on the type of raw data that comes solely from the score or from
auditory material can never account for the experiential aspect of the work
or the sense of recontextualization that I quoted from Dora A. Hanninen in
the Feldman chapter. Some kind of transformation has to take place through
extended listening. As we observed, materials re-presented aren't the same
things they were before, in the same way that a second repetition expresses
a difference as well as a similarity to the first.

The use of repetition and its relationship with memory also came up in
our discussion of Tsunoda's O Kokos Tis Anixis, in which each loop draws
us back into a procedure that has taken place previously and, in the process,
heightens our awareness of each moment as it unfolds. As Jennie highlighted
during our group discussion, Tsunoda employs various structural devices
across the different tracks:

Jennie: I was just going to say briefly, and this might be more
           parenthetical, but I do hear the Tsunoda tracks as having
           different functions within the work. So the first track is showing

the devices in a fairly condensed period of time, and there are others in there that show how little he can do while still maintaining the integrity of it. So a long track with very few loops, like two, or two and then a very small one or something, and then the final track being a bigger statement, doing more and going more places with them. I think there's something about an unfolding that happens through that technique.

Bryn: It's almost like a perceptual game at times, isn't it? If you've got 17 minutes, without any loops, it really plays with your sense of perception. At what point does that anticipation of a loop go away? I think for me, it never did. I kept hanging in there. And again, this, for me, points to the fact that these are compositions, rather than just treated field recordings, is the fact that just before the end of the track, he sticks a couple of loops back in.

Both Tsunoda and Feldman employ strategies designed to disorient the listener. These procedures, like the silences in the Szlavnics, served to heighten our awareness of the materials as they unfolded and helped draw us to the present-centeredness of these works. Each moment became imbued with the anticipation of what was directly to follow. In both of these works we found ourselves constantly questioning whether what we were listening to was a repeat of something previously heard or represented a new moment.

Similar perceptual difficulties were also observed in James Saunders' *511 possible mosaics*, through which instrumental lines became recontextualized to such a degree that they sounded to us, at times, like entirely new parts. I recall Jennie's surprise to find that each part in the score remains unchanged in each instance. The fact was that they never sounded exactly the same; different instrumental combinations would highlight registral changes or cause materials to get chunked in ways that lead to differing degrees of perceptual continuity. Some events appeared more linear than others; a closed-to-open mute position in a solo trombone version would convey a clearer sense of continuity than a muddied, lower-register multi-instrumental texture, for instance. The unchanging duration of the work accorded priority to form rather than content; through time we could anticipate the point of closure of each eighteen-second iteration while always grappling to come to terms with the multidimensional material of the work.

Duration

Jennie Gottschalk

The experience of duration is often described in terms of speed. A piece went by so slowly, or so quickly. The actual duration of a recording is simple enough to quantify. But how it feels in relation to that block of time is often a factor of the density of events within it. This density might be horizontal—such as a harmonic or timbral saturation—or vertical—in the speed of articulation and change—or both.

Depending on how duration is considered in *511 possible mosaics*, the density of events comes through quite differently. In our initial conversations about the duration of this work, we experienced some confusion due to the different premises of considering the whole recorded series and the individual segments. In both cases, though, there is the sense of things going by very quickly. The density of events is high. In one conversation I said, "It's interesting that that [duration] becomes somehow normalized, and you realize how much material is in those 18 or so seconds. It ends up feeling almost long once you're realizing how you have to engage with it, and all that's going on in there." All of us found that the duration itself became somewhat normalized after multiple iterations or multiple listenings. We were aware of the frame in which events occurred, and could begin to recognize how the material was operating in that frame, not unlike adjusting one's eyes in a dark room after a time. The much longer and unsegmented Möller example can only be tracked through listening that occurs on a broader scale. While those two extremes might be posed as concentration and patience, both qualities are potentially necessary in each case.

There is also a saturation point that can occur in different ways in this work. In vertical terms, the iterations are harder to grasp in their details when there are more instruments playing. This was referenced in the postlude to the Saunders.[3] But one key question is what actually constitutes the duration. Is it a single iteration, or the entirety of the performed set? Aside from the concentration required for close listening to a single iteration, some of us found it more difficult to concentrate after dozens of iterations had already occurred.[4] The ability to focus on the content became—at least for two of us—increasingly challenging over the second half of the total duration of the recording.

The sense of acclimation in the Spiegel, conversely, is not to a duration or form, but instead to an environment. In one of our conversations, when Bryn asked, "Jennie, do you think the Spiegel is a piece that has to be the length it is?" I immediately answered, "I think it could be 18 hours long. I'd be fine with that." The lack of segmentation of the work is part of what allows for that clear answer. The sense of being immersed in the sounds, rather than having to track or trace their configurations, is also part of that openness to a longer duration.

In the Ikeda, there was a similar openness due to the self-similarity of the material. In technical terms, the pieces might have been longer or shorter and still have had similar descriptions. As Bryn suggested of the Spiegel, "If you can extend it outwards forever, then it perhaps suggests that those proximities of events don't really matter, that it's just an ongoing thing." The difference in the Ikeda, particularly in my experience of it, was that the sheer physical intensity of it placed constraints on my endurance of its duration, though each track was rather short.

The Möller and Feldman examples present distinct durational challenges. The listening challenge of the Möller in this respect is on the macro-level—listening for very slow, directional change over time—while in the Feldman it occurs through shifting patterns that can only be observed at close range. There is no panoramic view of the Feldman that can be captured after the fact. It defies summary, but lives on in the memory through some recollection of its details.

When considering the question of whether this work could have been longer or shorter, Bryn said, "I think there is a shelf life to those pieces. There is a point when they do stop." The decision of when to end the piece was initially made by its composer, but perhaps is jointly intuited by its performers and listeners. The duration of the Möller is directly linked to its form: Events happen at a certain rate within a linear process until they have reached their logical conclusion. Like the Spiegel, though for very different reasons, the duration of Saunders' *511 possible mosaics* is almost incidental. It depends on the available instrumentation and possible combinations of the ensemble playing it. It would be about eighteen seconds long with one instrument, and about two and a half hours with all of them playing every possible combination.

Speed, velocity, and intensity

Richard Glover

Through surveying the chapters, postludes, and transcription of the discussion, we concluded that some pieces clearly suggest they are dealing with velocity more than others, seemingly using it as a tool in the creation process. Throughout the discussion, words such as speed and velocity were only used in consideration of the Ikeda tracks, which itself demonstrates that the methodology of initiating analytical discussion from the listening experience prompted a consideration of temporality through a wide variety of different lenses.

Speed was not the only lens through which temporality in the Ikeda was discussed. Jennie described how she felt that the Ikeda was the one track which *definitely* felt too long; she felt the tracks impacted her in a bodily way, and that she actually had a hard time being in the same room with them. Through the use of the high frequencies and the fast pulse, Ikeda uses high frequencies and a fast pulse to blend together velocity and intensity, which generates a challenge to endurance for the listener:

Richard: I think it might be an extreme example of endurance and
duration. After listening to them for a while, and after
repeated listens, you do get a sense of the physicality of them.
The materials in those tracks have a very specific spectral
makeup, they can cause very particular kinds of reactions. I
remember listening to one early on, and my eyes just started
to water just slightly—I was suddenly made aware of how my
sinuses are connected to everything else!

It seemed impossible for us to ignore the way in which our own bodies
experienced the vibrational qualities of these works.

An additional observation that we made was that the exposure effect, in
which repeated hearings afford the listener a greater predictive capability,
and thus more satisfaction from correct predictions, appeared not to apply
to our listening experience in relation to the Ikeda tracks. If, as listeners,
we experienced discomfort in terms of the bodily impact of the music, this
prompted further discomfort in repeated listenings. Correspondingly, rather
than achieving any sense of satisfaction, temporal flow seemed to grind to
a halt as the physical impact of the music, as opposed to the prediction of
future material, became the focal point of our experience.

Considerations of temporality and duration became about whether these
tracks need to be as long as they are:

Bryn: It reminds me of sitting through certain noise music
performances where physical level of tolerance is so much
a part of the experience. But it doesn't necessarily make me
think that that duration is too long, just that it makes me
think that it's too long *for me*. But I can sort of appreciate
that it's probably part of the intentionality of the music to
actually have to sit through that. It does raise some ethical
questions, but I suppose it raises questions connected with the
idea that there's still an obligation to go through those things.

However, later in the conversation, Bryn also remarked upon the duration
of these tracks in relation to intentionality:

Bryn: I thought the first two Ikeda tracks were probably a little
bit short, because I think there's something about having to
inhabit that sound world and become aware of things like
oscillation that takes time to really get inside that
Richard: Yes, they could be based around radio-edit length.
Bryn: I wasn't quite sure what kind of statement those tracks made
through being of a duration that I'd associate with a pop song
or something.

Both Jennie and I also remarked upon the fact that the specific choice
of speed and register had a discomforting effect on us as listeners. There

is an interesting link here with the fact that Ikeda's tracks are created in the studio, and as such it is clear that the audio is electronically generated; the listener has a particular relationship with this extreme material in that they do not *hear* human performers struggling to generate it. With the high-string clusters in Szlavnics' *Gradients of Detail*, we were able to experience the perceived strain of the players' bowing arms and close fingerings, which prompts a much closer relationship with the act of sound generation. I stated that the Ikeda was "more like a mirror or a sort of glossy surface, much more so than with an acoustic piece," in which, as a listener, I was further removed from attending to the act of sound generation within the music. This enabled me to "properly try to sense how much my listening processes were changing during the Ikeda." For me, this distance enabled an opportunity for a greater awareness of his listening approaches, and thus his temporal awareness.

Contrary to this idea, in Bryn's postlude to the Ikeda chapter he states that "[t]here appears to be something performative about these sweeps, as if the oscillation is being controlled by a human in real time, taking us somewhere." Bryn translated the sweeps into human gestures, seemingly "filling in" the distance between him as listener and the studio-based provenance of the audio material.

In both the Ikeda and the Saunders pieces, we all experienced information overload. Bryn stated in reference to the Ikeda that he didn't "really have much opportunity to exercise a sense of anticipation," "there's always the sort of sense of catching up," and when discussing the Saunders recalled "living slightly just behind what I'm listening to."

In Bryn's postlude to the Ikeda chapter, he mentions that he felt the music "operates at a speed which is beyond our immediate perception," and that "speed and directness make notions of the past largely redundant" to the point that: "I must listen and follow … to recollect is perhaps to miss the point …. I must follow its navigation and observe—rather than make sense of—its temporal flow." All of this was linked to the sense of intensity and speed arising from the Ikeda; I described the "relentlessness" of the pulse in his chapter on Ikeda, which Bryn aligned to a "machine-like insistence" in his postlude. In my chapter, I stated that the fast pulse rate prompted me to "focus upon the stability in that pulse rate, and [my] own perceived instability of that rate." I "found it almost impossible not to perceive change," while Bryn felt that "the pulses are of such speed and regularity that they almost become immobile, whilst the timbral aspect is active and subject to change." Here the informational overload seems to impress a transformational perception upon the original auditory material—a perceptual hallucination.

As an interesting counter to this position, in discussions of the beating speeds in the Szlavnics in which rate of the beats is often mentioned, these beating speeds do not seem to affect a broader sense of speed of experience throughout the piece; in our Szlavnics texts, neither Jennie nor I reference the issues of "catching up," as with the Ikeda. The occasional nature of the beats does not suggest an intensity throughout; they seem to emphasize the gradual shifts already occurring in the glissandi or sustained tones. In my chapter on Szlavnics' *Gradients of Detail*, I state that the "speeds of glissandi [and thus any beat patterns generated as a result of these glissandi] push temporal flow, but in recollection they are slower," certainly not a phenomenon experienced when we each reflected upon our experience of listening to the Ikeda. Speed of motion seems *very* different to speed in the listening, and thus speed in temporality as experienced.

Returning to the Ikeda, we all discussed how this intensity through velocity prompted a focus upon greater awareness of the local, and that the ability to switch to more of a macro-listening approach was more challenging when the pieces are shorter. The question was raised whether, if the Ikeda tracks were an hour long, we would develop a stronger ability to zoom out to a macro-listening. Bryn felt that we would have to, as the duration would demand it. This led onto discussion of the Saunders, relating to the quick pace of instrumental entries (although mentions of speed and rate are not brought up in Bryn's chapter) and the very short durational frames of the pieces. Additionally, here there was greater reference of textural density, and how intensity was heightened by this; in his chapter, Bryn spoke of the instruments "jostling" for space, the weight of the lower voices, heightened sense of textual interplay, and the dense layering of parts. All of this seemed to sharpen attention toward the intensity of these pieces.

The information overload was keenly perceived in the Saunders as well. Bryn remarked that "it's such an information overload, there's quite a strong sense of anticipation as well. I'm anticipating when that event's going to close and come to an end, simultaneously trying to make sense of what is happening at that given time." He points toward a sense of anticipation, but clearly just on the local level, an immediacy in detail, rather than on broader structural terms. How could he attempt to understand a broader sense of the entire structure, when the individual pieces are each so short?

However, there are clearly points within the Saunders in which variation in our experience occurs. Bryn's Saunders chapter mentions him being "struck by the relatively relaxed pace of the music, and a pronounced sense of having 'slowed down'. There was no sense of competing for space and phrases had the opportunity to breathe." He talks of the Saunders stretching and elongating, but rarely do any of us directly refer to *speed* in the Saunders when describing our temporal experience, but rather how density and texture vary.

This sense of always being behind, of not being able to perceive and comprehend what is being heard, resulted in what Bryn defined as a "sense of frustration," echoed by Jennie. Bryn felt the Feldman was a useful opposition here, as "it's much slower. There's time for me to absorb and listen. And with the Szlavnics, the Spiegel and Möller, there's that sense of inhabiting a world that makes certain demands on me as a listener, but also gives me the opportunity to reflect." Interestingly, Jennie didn't group the Feldman in the same way here:

> The one that I question more in that sense is the Feldman, just because there are so many small events that are different from each other, so I'm often trying to split those things apart.

Jennie is suggesting here that she found there *isn't* much time to reflect in the Feldman because of the numerous local level events occurring. In his listening commentary, Bryn actually aligns with this, as "the music is wholly reliant upon memory and yet, with its insistence on each moment, offers no real opportunity to reflect."

Through our discussions, it is clear that this lack of ability to reflect, or lack of awareness of "space," doesn't specifically relate to speed, but points toward an awareness of durational frame, and how current material might fit within that. Ultimately, how much clarity can the listener gain from the broader structure? The sense of disorientation in the Feldman comes from the secure knowledge gained early on that the structure will comprise of confusing, disruptive sequences of materials throughout; Bryn said he was encouraged to "stop making sense of things and simply listen." This is similar to the experience of listening to the disruptive loops in the Tsunoda. Jennie stated how she listened explicitly for variation in the Tsunoda, due to the nature of the loops.

However, the notion of "space" was mentioned far more often in discussions of pieces with slower speeds, such as the Spiegel (who Jennie quotes as describing her own work as "slow change music"), the Möller, and clearly in moments in the Feldman, despite the contrasting comments from Bryn and Jennie describing the lack of ability to reflect and being prompted to listen, or parse material. *The Expanding Universe* was described through analogies of flight (Jennie) and clouds (Richard); the notion of space, thus affording the ability to reflect and gain awareness of one's own listening attitude, arises broadly from the gradual development of structural understanding in slower, longer pieces.

Are there initial signals to zoom out and attempt to understand the structure of these pieces? What material, if any, is impacting upon these initial signals? A specific rate of change cannot be objectively defined in the material, as our chapters show that rates of change can come from slower, longer-form structures (Feldman), steady organ drones which envelop and fill the space or listener (Möller), or steady-state pulsing (Ikeda). I observed that the speed of the pulses presented in the Ikeda is not directly related to temporal flow rate.

An apparent link between the Ikeda and the Spiegel that arose from these considerations is the continued stability of the two tracks, which seems to exist as a consequence of the electronically generated nature of their material. I referenced the "surface" in the Ikeda, and that in the Spiegel:

> You know that each onset or pulse echo is going to be basically the same dynamic, and it's going to be sounded the same, and you can only get that kind of precision through electronics. That's one of the things that makes the Feldman so interesting. You know that obviously he's going to change dynamics, but also that the performers are necessarily going to be changing.

I went on to say:

> Bryn, everything that you were saying about hearing the breath, the point is, the majority of these pieces all have very reductive materials in comparison to other music, and so those elements are being magnified significantly, and are much more perceptible. So I think even though the Ikeda and the Spiegel are quite different in terms of the way they're made, there perhaps isn't the sense of being pulled through. It's like not being performed at, or having something presented at me, which I have when I sense the players.

Jennie agreed, adding that "for me, they're more like being stuck alone in a room alone with my own thoughts, versus being in some sort of dynamic."

The speed and brevity of the Ikeda tracks prevented each of us from being able to reflect, and from accessing the sense of space that was so easily found in some of the other pieces. However, the studio environment apparent within the auditory material of Ikeda's work (and also Spiegel's) allowed each of us to remain at a distance to the local-level material. This constituted a contrast to the way that we felt our perceived temporalities were pushed along by hearing the actions of the human performers in the Feldman, Saunders and Szlavnics pieces.

Subjectivity

Jennie Gottschalk

We have written in the introduction that this book deals in the specific— the encounters of individual people with individual works and with each other—rather than with generalities. Musical temporality can only be judged through subjective experience. However much we may reflect upon an individual piece from multiple perspectives, our observations are necessarily rooted in subjective experience. In this context, we cannot address the works for their objective musical qualities alone, but also have to consider the conditions they set up for individual experience. To conclude the chapter, we will briefly consider the major subjective factors we have identified through our experiences of these works.

Our experience of each work is directly impacted by how much we know about it, either from prior listening experiences or through information gleaned from each other's writing, other written material, or a contextual knowledge of related work. When we have a sense of what parameters are most at play, we can direct our attention to those behaviors and more quickly identify their impact. Conversely, approaching a work with an open mind, as a blank slate, might allow a different set of opportunities for a listener to take it on its own terms and discover unfamiliar modes of operation or types of impact.

More specifically, the memory of a work, whether in prior moments or prior listenings, directs attention and helps to shape experience from moment to moment. Memory was discussed in the earlier section of this chapter on form, and also plays a role in our anticipation of the how the work will reveal itself over time. This anticipation can also be encouraged through pattern recognition, such as the glissandi in the Szlavnics or the pulsations of the Ikeda. We have discussed how the Feldman is constantly interfering with the patterns it suggests, which creates a complicated dynamic around anticipation. The form of the Möller creates a clear sense of anticipation throughout the work, but only once it is known.

The next set of subjective factors circle around the choice and capacity for engagement: concentration, patience, and endurance. The Feldman, Saunders, and Szlavnics works all demand a close attention to details that shift from moment to moment. Patience is often a factor in the reception of longer works, such as the Möller and the Spiegel. It also comes into play with the shifts in form and long absences of looping in some tracks of the Tsunoda set. Endurance is related to intensity, whether of pulsation and amplitude in the Ikeda or the demand of the Feldman for concentration over a long period of time.

Another set of concerns is best presented through a visual analogy of zoom level. This relates to concentration, but is a particular aspect of it. It is also related to speed, and as such is discussed in the previous section. At what level of detail is the listener being asked to pay attention? I recalled that after my first experience of a Morton Feldman work, *Coptic Light* (1986), many years ago, I questioned whether this was music to be listened to very closely or put on in the background. While it has certainly been used in both ways, Feldman's work demands and rewards a close, even myopic, level of attention. That is certainly true of *Piano, Violin, Viola, Cello*.

In the Tsunoda, the zoom level shifts according to the content of the field recordings, and primarily through the frequency and behavior of the loops. The Spiegel and Möller works, despite their formal differences, both seem to invite an immersive listening experience that is less differentiated from moment to moment. In the Saunders, attention is demanded at an effectively microscopic level to track the shifts in instrumentation and gather information about an elusive totality.

The final aspect of subjectivity that we would like to highlight might be termed "self-awareness of self-reflection," or "listening to oneself listening." Silence is often a trigger for this kind of process, such as the long pauses we experienced in the Szlavnics. Loops that have a long duration often have a similar impact in the Tsunoda. The sparsity of audible change in the Möller and Spiegel pieces also invite a self-reflective process, often leading to thought on topics outside of music. Conversely, the density of information and frequency of change in the Saunders and Feldman pieces present a challenge to the faculty of listening that can lead to a more musically based introspection.

These responses are highly personal; and yet we have found meaningful points of resonance among our three experiences of these works. It is both possible and useful to analyze these subjective aspects of experience in relation to musical traits. We have found that we can best understand the pairing of musical behaviors with subjective responses through a listening practice that is analytical, introspective, and deeply collaborative. Our numerous conversations about multiple experiences of the same set of works have had a significant impact on each of the authors' musical thinking. The inclusion of subjectivity as a part of those discussions has been both central and illuminating.

*** *** ***

All of these musical and subjective factors (form, repetition, duration, speed, intensity, knowledge, memory, concentration, etc.) are interlinked and interdependent. Some connections are obvious, but it is useful to unpack them and find the contradictions, both to common knowledge—i.e., the assumption that short pieces require less endurance—and among our individual reactions. While it was tempting to simply talk about the works and let our multiple experiences and reactions speak for themselves, the focus in this chapter on the behaviors and their subjective results offers a set of propositions for further engagement with the topic of temporality. As this work is done, and particularly as it is done collaboratively, other contradictions, behaviors, and reactions will emerge and affect musical practice. Some reflections on the methodology for doing so are discussed in the following chapter.

Notes

1   See page 140.
2   See page 165.
3   See page 64.
4   See page 64.

Epilogue

There was no precedent that we were aware of for a book written collaboratively about listening practices. While we had planned to write chapters based upon specific pieces and then involve group discussion to reflect on material, ideas, and perspectives brought up in those chapters, a larger overall structure grew organically through ongoing discussion. Although we all felt that the starting point for the book had to be our own personal responses to the pieces we had selected, a structure slowly emerged that revealed a "hall of mirrors" approach. By including the postlude sections and following up with in-depth discussions, each of us was able to reflect back on the other authors' chosen tracks, and on our own responses to those pieces. At the end of this process, we have come to realize that our reflection has not only been on the musical works but on each of us as subjects. Most essentially, encounters between the three of us—as listeners and as people—have shaped the content of the book.

Rather than exploring a range of works by a given composer, which we felt would only lead to a more generalized apprehension of the music, we found that focusing on specific pieces gave us more to say. Each piece, taken on its own terms, revealed more and more with each listening. This is reflected in each of the chapters and postludes which explore, specifically, our perceptions of the behaviors of each specific piece. In some cases, the writing style of individual chapters mirrored the musical structures of the pieces. In Bryn's chapter on Morton Feldman's *Piano, Violin, Viola, Cello*, his analytical voice and his perceptual voice engage in a dialogue with one another that leads the reader to constantly readjust their focus, and to repeatedly recontextualize their understanding of his observations. The writing style reflects the nature of Feldman's piece, which constantly reintroduces heard materials in new contexts. Similarly, Jennie's "Monoliths" chapter has long journalistic passages and extended, highly subjective reflections that mirror her experience of the two works under discussion. The Tsunoda chapter is sectional, corresponding to the eight distinct tracks of the work and the shifts, breaks, and stoppages within most of the tracks. Richard's chapter on Chiyoko Szlavnics' *Gradients of Detail* pulls apart different sonic and performative parameters and discusses them individually in discrete sections. This approach relates to the block-like structure of the piece itself, which moves from solo line, to cluster, to silence and back throughout.

The methodology of continual engagement and re-engagement with the particular pieces and each other's perspectives on them helped us build up our own languages of temporality surrounding each piece. Discussion became centered upon multiple specificities, and how we were able to explore our individual responses to single pieces alongside each other. Through continuous discussion on a more localized level, we became proficient at homing in on relevant issues.

Having three authors involved in the project proved especially potent for this process, as the postludes were summaries of the discussion between two of us, on the *other* writer's chapter. Thus, the process prevented the same comments continually recurring, and enabled fresh perspectives and ideas to arise at all levels of discussion and writing. The initial focus of our individual chapters upon specific pieces then expanded to a broader consideration of musical behaviors in Chapter 7; observations pertaining to individual experiences, of individual pieces, were then juxtaposed with appropriate observations from other pieces, in order to reveal more about both. In this way, the overall methodology of a highly specific approach in the chapters, moving through different forms of reflection into more global observations, revealed detailed links, similarities, differences and insights into how we experience and understand temporality.

In the final stages of this intensive reflective process, we find ourselves considering its potential utility for the reader as a template for similar investigations. Our process has been outlined in the introduction, but a more open form of it could include various iterations and cycles of theme and piece selection, listening, written reflection, and group discussion. This basic approach could be—and perhaps already is—undertaken in educational settings, among colleagues, or informally among friends with an active shared interest. It depends primarily on careful listening and an openness to the ensuing dialogue. The application of this kind of process can—based on our experience—reveal aspects of the topic, the works, and the participants that would be unlikely to otherwise come to light.

The changing experiences that we bring to our listening across several days or months or years are such that the book can't reach a conclusion, but is part of an ongoing changing perception for each of its authors. These ongoing, in-depth conversations about musical temporality with others who are also deeply engaged in the topic are a catalyst for a deepening view of the subject and of our own subjectivities; we have had significant mutual influence on each other. It has become clear to us that the more we explore each piece and draw relationships between ideas, the more there is to say. Specific, fully engaged musical experiences are not abstract exercises, but actual experiences. They have an impact on perception outside of their listening radius and duration. We carry them with us into our lives and into the world. The musical experiences we choose have the potential to change us. When we immerse ourselves in them, they offer potential ways of inhabiting a duration that are possible in the broader temporal canvas of our day-to-day experience.

Appendix: Suggested Further Reading and Listening

What follows is a selection of recommendations that we would like to share with the reader. The suggestions given by each author` are by no means comprehensive and do not attempt to provide full scholarly accounts of the many excellent publications available on temporality in music, literature, psychology, philosophy, and the arts. Instead what we offer are brief reflections on some of the books, articles, and compositions that have inspired each of us to think differently or more deeply about temporality. Each of these texts and selected pieces of music have challenged our assertions, and, in the process, solidified existing lines of inquiry. It is hoped that these suggestions will illuminate and give voice to our individual contributions to the book as well as providing the reader with examples of work that may inform, provoke, question, and perhaps further their own understanding of temporal issues.

Bryn Harrison

My recommendations are taken from poetry, philosophy, and music and reflect a personal interest in temporality that goes back over twenty years. My fascination with the subject of time came not through music but from the poetry of Octavio Paz (1914–98). As the former Mexican Ambassador for India (1962–68), Paz became steeped in Buddhist culture and this is endlessly reflected through his poetry in which he constantly alludes to the present-centeredness of experience, often expressed through the dissolution of differences. This is encapsulated in Paz's poem, "As One Listens to the

Rain": "*Listen to me as one listens to the rain/not attentive, not distracted.*"[1] While Paz may seem like an unlikely inclusion here, I would argue that his work elegantly conveys the inseparability of time and being expressed elsewhere in this book.

The inseparability of time and being is also expressed in Maurice Merleau-Ponty's seminal text *Phenomenology of Perception*. Here he states that "consciousness constitutes time"[2] and that "we must understand time as the subject and the subject as time."[3] I feel a certain empathy here to his view, having written elsewhere that "time cannot be intellectualised or understood in an empirical sense since this requires us to objectify time."[4] These statements echo the objectives of the book.

Having included a chapter on my perceptual responses to Morton Feldman's late work, *Piano, Violin, Viola, Cello*, I would like to recommend here some of the excellent recordings available of his late works. Nearly all of these works are long in duration and, I would argue, deal with the kinds of temporal issues—particularly those of memory and repetition—expressed in my chapter. The Aki Takahashi and the Kronos Quartet's recording of *Piano and String Quartet*[5] was the first disc of Feldman's music that I heard and is one that I still record as a landmark recording. I would also regard the HatHut recordings made by the Ives Ensemble as excellent choices for those not already familiar with Feldman's late works. While earlier releases are now more difficult to obtain, the HatHut catalogue has since expanded to include recordings of *Trio*, *For John Cage*, *Three Voices*, *Patterns in a Chromatic Field*, and *Triadic Memories*. I would also recommend the impressive Another Timbre recording of *Piano, Violin, Viola, Cello*.[6]

Of the growing number of excellent publications on Feldman's work, I would like to draw attention in particular to Dora A Hanninen's article, *Feldman, Analysis, Experience*,[7] in which she puts forward the view that "analysis is an investigation of experience," and addresses "the challenges of scale" in *Coptic Light* and "the challenges of repetition" in *Piano, Violin, Viola, Cello*. This paper in particular deepened my understanding of Feldman's work and had some bearing on how I approached the writing in my particular chapter.

I would also like to recommend Aldo Clementi's music as an example of a composer that has dealt very explicitly with temporal issues. I have written elsewhere of my first experience of hearing Clementi's music, expressing, "I became more and more immersed in a musical continuum, a form that seemed to suggest a permanent state of becoming that simultaneously drew me into the very fabric of the music."[8] Much of Clementi's output exemplifies this approach and the six tracks presented on the Ricordi disc *Capriccio*[9] and the Ives ensemble's 1999 release *Madrigale*.[10]

Jennie Gottschalk

Since the focus of my research has been largely on practitioners and on the conceptual linkages among their works, my recommendations for further reading will relate more strongly to practice than to theory. For a wealth of suggestions for creative strategies, an unlikely but very rich source is the chapter called "The Perception of Time," in William James' *The Principles of Psychology, vol. 1*. In *Experimental Music Since 1970*, I included a section called "The Perception of Time" (pages 133–147), which discusses various approaches to this issue, with only a partial overlap with the material in this book. In that section I suggest that visual art is a frequent source of both inspiration and guidance, in particular when time in music is understood as analogous to space in art. The field of visual art is suggestive of any number of further musical experiments, and I have no doubt that there are analogies to draw with other art forms that might be equally productive.

As much as my own frame of reference has centered on experimental music for the past decade or so, the subject of temporality in music is vast, and can be explored in reference to any number of traditions and categories. Musicians who have related themselves to Afrofuturism are particularly interesting to me in this context. Camae Ayewa's *Black Quantum Futurism Soundwaves*[11] are sonic illustrations of the ideas explored in *Black Quantum Futurism: Theory & Practice, vol. 1* (2015), edited by Rasheedah Phillips, and is one of several possible entry points into her modes of temporal innovation. *Fetish Bones* (2016), released under her name Moor Mother Goddess, is described as "an album intended as a form of protest and also as [a] form of time travel—a collection of sounds that are events themselves, telling stories rich in history about the journey that brings us to today and the future we are creating."[12] Sun Ra is an iconic Afrofuturist, and his *Space Is the Place* (1974) film is a vivid introduction to his work and thought. Erik Steinskog's *Afrofuturism and Black Sound Studies: Culture, Technology, and Things to Come* (2018) includes ample discussion of the functions of memory and imagination in the work he introduces. Like "experimental music," the term "Afrofuturism" is not universally or uncritically accepted by the people to whom it is attached. But it is alluring in the context of this book because of the temporal implications embedded within it and because its invitation to consider the role of time in the many genres it includes.

The necessity that has been elaborated in Afrofuturist thought of reinventing or reimagining the past and imagining new futures lends new light to the idea of the present. William James brought the idea of "the specious present" into circulation in the chapter I mentioned above, relating the notion of a duration block to "a bow and a stern, as it were—a rearward—and a forward-looking end." He writes, "We seem to feel the interval of time as a whole, with its two ends embedded in it."[13] The "moment form" that Jonathan Kramer writes about with initial reference to Stockhausen's writings and music is conversely reliant upon discontinuity.[14] These multiple approaches to the present are fascinating to me. Among other possibilities, it can be extended through stasis, verticalized through sectionality, or transformed through the reimagining of past and future.

Richard Glover

My own reference points for temporal experience began with an interest in Ligeti's micropolyphonic works such as *Lontano*, which avoids clear sectional demarcation through continuous streams of narrow, linear patterns. When I came into contact with the sustained tone music of Phill Niblock, Charlemagne Palestine, and Alvin Lucier, these continuous sound environments provided rich sources of experiences for exploring my own subjective temporalities. While attending the Ostrava Days institute in 2005, I heard Lucier discussing his interest in how beating patterns created their own pulses and phrases, and thus how pitch can become rhythm. Since then, I have held a deep interest in the way that pitch, harmony, and sonority can generate such vividly different temporal experiences in listeners. Éliane Radigue's electronic works, in particular her *Trilogie de la Mort* from 1985 to 1993, brought an extraordinary new dimension due to the exquisitely crafted glacial rate of change within the music.

Don Ihde's 1976 phenomenological study *Listening and Voice*[15] employs bold writing with such a high level of clarity to describe his own individual, subjective auditory experience, rather than with reference to any other external source. I sensed a sincerity in attempting to understand the personal nature of experiencing, an approach also manifested in the 1983 publication of Thomas Clifton's *Music as Heard*,[16] which similarly attempts a phenomenological study into how we hear, process, and understand music from a listener's perspective. Likewise, while the vast majority of Jonathan Kramer's 1988 book *The Time of Music*[17] draws upon a score-based analysis of proportion and duration, Chapter 12.2 details a highly personalized experience with Satie's *Vexations*. The nature of this writing departs significantly from the numerical-based analytic approach in other chapters and—similar to the Ihde and Clifton—demonstrates a keenness and candour in attempting to understand temporality as experienced during the listening process.

Finally, I have taken much inspiration from the work of philosopher Alva Noë, who argues in *Action in Perception*[18] that we should consider the role of our perception in terms of the sense of touch: a haptic approach to perceiving the world. Our perceptual systems are in an active state of "reaching out" to the world, and I find the metaphorical use of this framework for the listener to music as a very insightful strategy. The cellist Charles Curtis' comments that the audience to Lucier's music as placed in a sort of "performing posture,"[19] as they listen out for the sonic detail in the sound, align with this notion; we as listeners are responsible for our own listening strategies.

Notes

1   Octavio Paz, *Collected Poems 1957–1987* (Manchester: Carcanet Press, 1998), 615.

2   Maurice Merleau-Ponty, *Phenomenology of Perception* (London: Routledge, 1962), 414.

3   Ibid., 422.

4   Richard Glover and Bryn Harrison, *Overcoming Form, Reflections on Immersive Listening* (Huddersfield: U of Huddersfield Press, 2013), 42.

5   *Piano and String Quartet,* Elektra Nonesuch 9 79320-2, 1993.

6   *Piano, Violin, Viola, Cello,* Another Timbre at113, 2017.

7   Dora A. Hanninen, "Feldman, Analysis, Experience," *Twentieth-Century Music* 1, no. 2 (2004): 225.

8   Bryn Harrison, "The Tempo of Enclosed Spaces; A Short, Personal Reflection on the Ensemble Music of Aldo Clementi," *Contemporary Music Review* 30, nos 3–4 (2011): 269–274.

9   *Capriccio,* Agorá 1004, 1999.

10   *Madrigale,* hat[now]ART 123, 1999.

11   "Black Quantum Futurism Soundwaves," https://blackquantumfuturism.bandcamp.com/album/black-quantum-futurism-soundwaves

12   "Fetish Bones," https://moormothergoddess.bandcamp.com/album/fetish-bones

13   William James, *The Principles of Psychology, v. 1* (New York: Dover, 1950), 609–610.

14   Jonathan Kramer, *The Time of Music: New Meanings, New Temporalities, New Listening Strategies* (New York: Schirmer, 1988), 201–220.

15   Don Ihde, *Listening and Voice: Phenomenologies of Sound* (New York: State University of New York Press, 1976)

16   Thomas Clifton, *Music as Heard: Study in Applied Phenomenology* (New Haven, CT: Yale University Press, 1983).

17   Jonathan Kramer, *The Time of Music: New Meanings, New Temporalities, New Listening Strategies* (New York: Schirmer, 1988).

18   Alva Noë, *Action in Perception* (Cambridge, MA: MIT Press, 2004).

19   Charles Curtis, "Alvin Lucier: A Performer's Notes," *Leonardo Music Journal* 22 (2012). Online supplement. http://www.mitpressjournals.org/doi/abs/10.1162/LMJ_a_00111. Accessed November 6, 2013.

INDEX